M000309867

ENTER ASSISI

Enter Assisi

An Invitation to
FRANCISCAN
SPIRITUALITY

MURRAY BODO

franciscan
media
Cincinnati, Ohio

Scripture passages have been taken from *New Revised Standard Version Bible,* copyright ©1989 by the Division of Christian Education of the National Council of the Churches of Christ in the U.S.A., and used by permission. All rights reserved. Scripture quotations noted NLT are taken from the *Holy Bible,* New Living Translation, copyright ©1996, 2004, 2007. Used by permission of Tyndale House Publishers, Inc., Carol Stream, Illinois 60188. All rights reserved.

Cover design by Candle Light Studios
Cover image © Shutterstock
Book design by Mark Sullivan

LIBRARY OF CONGRESS CATALOGING-IN-PUBLICATION DATA
Bodo, Murray.
Enter Assisi : an invitation to Franciscan spirituality / Murray Bodo.
pages cm
ISBN 978-1-61636-709-1 (alk. paper)
1. Christian pilgrims and pilgrimages—Italy—Assisi. 2. Francis, of Assisi, Saint, 1182-1226. I. Title.
BX2321.A8B63 2015
263'.04245651—dc23
2014038013

ISBN 978-1-61636-709-1

Copyright ©2015, Murray Bodo. All rights reserved.

Published by Franciscan Media
28 W. Liberty St.
Cincinnati, OH 45202
www.FranciscanMedia.org

Dedication

. . .

WHEN I WAS YOUNG AND EAGER AND NO PLACE WAS A PLACE TOO far, I came at last to Assisi. At last, because I had dreamed of that mystical city, its gates, its walls, its hillside perch, from the age of thirteen when I first met St. Francis in a book that became more important than the travel and adventure books I was then reading, books that took me to places exotic and dangerous. At last, because in that first book about St. Francis the image of the young Francis standing beside one of the city gates waiting for his father's return, captured my imagination. Who was this young man? Where had his father been?

To answer those questions I began a quest that finally found its grail when I was thirty-five years old. Thirty-five! *Nel mezzo del cammin di nostra vita*—in the middle of the road of our life— as Dante has it at the beginning of the *Divine Comedy.* Dante found himself through a dark wood and wild, and I refound myself through a journey back in time to the mountain town of Assisi in the province of Umbria in the heart of central Italy.

I was brought to a new wholeness in Assisi. This is my book of thanksgiving for those three months when I let the city, the people, the very air heal me. I dedicate *Enter Assisi* to the people of Assisi.

Contents

. . .

Foreword

...

ENTER ASSISI IS A BEAUTIFUL BOOK. IT IS A POET'S BOOK. IT IS a sensitive, careful recollection of days and occurrences and instances that soothe and comfort, not unlike stroking the fur of a dog sitting next to you on a veranda in the afternoon. That is what this book was like for me, a comfortable place to return to, something I picked up over and over again, sometimes only reading a few words, sometimes an entire page or chapter. The images captivated my attention and took me back to the cobblestone streets and the rock walls of a town I, too, love—Assisi.

I have looked through many travel books and guides since I lived there forty years ago, but the images fall flat. Though certainly picturesque and alluring in its medieval charm, as many Italian hill towns are, Assisi is so much more! Photographs of Assisi show only the two-dimensional, like postcards that you pick up and mail or take home with you to look at; they are just one view, one perspective of the image taken. *Enter Assisi* is like walking inside the photograph, using the image as a door or gate and sitting comfortably inside while a great writer's eye takes you on a journey.

I know this because the pages of this book take me there, but also because of my own journey nearly forty years ago to the places Murray Bodo speaks of here. He brings to life again what I saw and felt during the months I lived in Assisi and adds another layer of insight that brings me closer once again to the holiness of that place, and for that I am grateful.

I was a college student when I first went to Assisi. I had just lost my father *and* was also an injured, pain-ridden varsity athlete who had been looking forward to a career in sports when a gymnastics accident occurred that broke my neck and back. The physical pain was excruciating, but so was the spiritual pain of feeling abandoned by God. I felt I had lost not only my dad, but with the accident, that I'd lost myself as I knew me to be—a cocky tomboy who loved nature and hiking in the hills, all things sport, and animals—I loved animals. In the midst of my grief, a friend gave me a copy of Murray Bodo's *Francis: The Journey and the Dream*, and it was then that I met Francis and realized that I, like him, had grown up in a small mountain town, loved the same wild creatures, and had my own battles and visions to fight. Would I win or lose?

After a year of suffering weekly trips to a pain control center, I announced to my doctors that I was leaving for a while—that I had to go and talk to St. Francis. They, of course, thought I was crazy, but then a lot of people thought St. Francis was crazy, too. But when I stood at the bottom of the hill, on the train platform in Santa Maria degli Angeli, and looked up at Assisi shining on the side of Mount Subasio, I took off my soft-collar neck support, threw my sling for my partially paralyzed right arm into a nearby trash can, and knew I was home. There, thousands of miles away from everyone and everything I had known, I felt more at home than in any other place I had been to. Assisi has a way of doing that to people.

And that is the Assisi I found again in this book, a place come alive on the page, beyond the page. Murray Bodo's writing adds the third dimension—you enter into another world: his world.

This book is a memoir of Murray Bodo's Assisi, the life-giving nuances of the streets, the sounds, the people, and meaningful relationships with places and things that enrich our existence. He has a way of transforming the ordinary to the sublime. Murray Bodo can take a small hill town and write of it as if it is Paris, France. He takes the poverty of a thirteenth-century saint and draws a richness from it that makes sense to our hectic modern world, brings comfort and insight—that is the beauty and the wealth of this book to be found by any reader who will take the time to savor the wisdom in the tales, to linger on its pages, and *Enter Assisi...*

—Susan Saint Sing, Ph.D.

author of *A Pilgrim in Assisi*

Acknowledgments

. . .

My heartfelt thanks to Dr. Susan Saint Sing for her creative ideas and for her invaluable help with background material and color, and to my editors at Franciscan Media, Diane M. Houdek and Kathleen M. Carroll.

Introduction

. . .

INVITATION

As with a friend grown so close we can no longer see each other objectively, so has Assisi grown familiar to me. I return again and again, and she is still there, still dear, but without her first beautiful revelation of something more I wanted to be near, something more I wanted to discover. One can only have that first extraordinary experience once, and all the rest is going back trying to remember that first glow, trying to hold onto it, trying to enter it again. My first experience of Assisi was like that of one of the children in C.S. Lewis's *The Lion, the Witch, and the Wardrobe*. I had gone into the wardrobe and out the other side into a lovely, magical world that took me out of myself into the world of St. Francis.

I see this searching, this hope for transformation, transcendence, in the eyes of many pilgrims who walk through Assisi's gates to this day. People come to the edge of Assisi because they are looking for something; they enter in hoping to find what they seek. Some, like me, come back again and again, some can only come once in a lifetime. And I believe that for many the rocks and stones do speak, and most leave with something they didn't have before. Assisi leaves its mark on those who enter it.

Not even a casual tourist leaves without an indelible impression of the Middle Ages come alive in the twenty-first century. But to the true seeker, the one who comes as a pilgrim does, for a purpose, for healing, for answers, for grace, Assisi becomes the intermediary. The story of Francis and Clare is in every stone, every shop window. What you bring of your own story continues the tale.

For me, even now over forty years after we met, forty years of yearly pilgrimages to Assisi, it still retains something more that I cannot seem to hold onto, some mystery that is like the mystery even the closest friend still preserves as her or his own. Our tale together is not finished yet. And so I continue to try to say what I can't really say, reveal what I really can't reveal. The mystery remains: a part of the uniqueness of the other and of my own response to the other. The other is a town and more than a town, an experience that continues to draw me, though I struggle to find words to say what that is.

What I do know, and what I have experienced with certainty, is that the decision to go to Assisi, to walk through the gates that lead you in can be one of the greatest entries of a lifetime. It can be life altering, life changing. Myriad events will follow along the footsteps and paths, niches and alleys that you cross, but the first step, the entering through the gates is the most important. It is my hope that through writing about the gates, the stones, the noises and sounds inside the city, the historical dimensions—in short, what I have seen, experienced, and learned over half my lifetime—will bring Assisi to life for you, and the joy of St. Francis will skip the stones with you.

Perhaps these chapters woven together will say more than they say individually; perhaps all these gates entered and exited together will tell more than any one could do alone. Walls and gates, people and chapters, after all, are meant to be understood in context. The whole is greater than the sum of its parts. Even so, the parts have to be experienced individually to understand the whole they become.

Something like that is what kept me writing this book. A desire from deep within me to share and tell, like someone looking across the Grand Canyon for the first time, or seeing a glacier in the Alps, or a whale sounding in the North Atlantic—I want to share with you what I have seen and experienced. What isn't here in all these pages taken together, is what I still couldn't find words for on each individual page. My hope is that you who read these pages will supply what is missing by going yourself to Assisi, entering her gates, staying there awhile, and leaving with more than you imagined when you first set out to know more about this city on a hill that the Italians call, "La Città Mistica," the Mystical City. If you have been to Assisi, these pages will evoke places once experienced and never forgotten. And if you cannot go to Assisi, perhaps in these pages you can hear me whisper to you what the stones and the sun and the stars have whispered to me, and you will travel there in your imagination and experience inside the words what you cannot experience by going across the sea to Assisi. Perhaps the words themselves will take you to your own mystical city.

Part One

ENTER ASSISI

Chapter One

...

ASSISI IS...

ASSISI IS A TOWN SLAPPED ON THE SIDE OF A MOUNTAIN, SO THAT every morning when I wake up I am either looking down over the valley of Spoleto or looking up at Mount Subasio. That is a given. Another given is the air. The air is always cool and crisp in the morning. No matter what temperature Brother Sun takes the midday to, the morning air is fresh and cool. It is this air that I breathe deeply as I write. It is taking notice of the elements, as St. Francis did—earth, water, air, and fire—that allows you to stay close to the Creator and to the spiritual dimension of Assisi, the town of St. Francis, because without holding these elements close, you can easily find yourself engulfed in the Assisi of Pietro Bernardone—the wealthy cloth merchant—St. Francis's father! Assisi is home to both, nestles them both.

Assisi is the city inside the rumble and chatter of cars and people. Assisi is built on the slopes of Mount Subasio whose summit is 4,229 feet above sea level. The city is set longitudinally from southwest to northeast along overlapping natural terraces. Its houses are made of stone quarried from Mount Subasio that turns red in the warm light of sunset and pale under moonlight. The doorways often have an ogival shape (pointed, as in Gothic arches) and are usually made of stone. The roofs are of terra cotta tiles and hang over the streets; they are sustained by wooden corbels. Geraniums bloom on windowsills and balconies.

Assisi is a city that shines forth, even from the greed of commerce, the veneer of shops not unlike the cloth shop of Pietro Bernardone. It shines in the faces of young mothers who parade their babies like Lady Pica cradling her young Francesco as she and Pietro make their way to church.

Assisi is the face that draws crowds of pilgrims and enables them to endure the crush of the crowds, the booming "Silenzio" from loudspeakers inside the basilica that houses the tomb of the Silent One, where the Little Poor Man's hidden bones lie yellowing inside the sarcophagus that seems to shine like polished Assisi stone.

Assisi is the spirit of Francis who continues to live inside everything he left for his great love, Jesus, but then reentered when Jesus revealed to him that he is inside everything we give up for love of him.

Assisi is the face of God who is there inside and outside of everything that exists and that we foolishly try to possess. We cannot possess it; we must simply allow ourselves to be held by it.

Assisi is what Francis gave up when he walked out of its gates, freeing it from anyone's possession and making it everyone's desire: the desire to walk the streets of a paradise we cannot own but only visit while we walk the earth. It becomes ours only when we let it be what it is: the dwelling place of the Poor Man, Francis, who gave it up so that we could see how the Spirit lives in what has been freely given back to God.

Assisi is the pilgrim heart of the human heart that journeys toward God. Assisi is the city whose stone gates begin to shine when we leave them behind and let them lead us back into the world made beautiful by the spirit of poverty we've learned in this holy city whose flowers in window boxes and on balconies make us see beautiful flowers everywhere.

Assisi is a second home to me. To be back here now over forty years after I first woke to this same silence; to be here opening the shutters in the morning dark to the static of lights in the valley below. There the dome of Santa Maria degli Angeli (St. Mary of the Angels) stands watch over the Porziuncola, the small chapel where Francis made a fitting space for the brothers to be fed by the Word of God and the bread of the Holy Eucharist.

To wake again in the silence of that darkness before the light of dawn, before the birds awake, before the bells start ringing, before the first rumblings of cars and rattle of feet and voices on the cobblestone streets of Assisi. To lean out the window and feel the moon wash you clean of the night's demons and nightmares. Or staying awake, to lie on the ground of the roof garden of Casa Papa Giovanni where I've lived so many years of summers and falls, letting the moon whiten what the noonday sun had turned brown, praying for a moon shower that, like a baptismal rush of water, will satisfy the yearning for purification, for holiness.

To imagine Clare in her dormitory in San Damiano outside the city walls seeing the same silent darkness trembling with the breathing of her sleeping sisters—and Francis and his brothers farther still down the slope of the hill, awake or asleep on their wattled mats or on the cold ground waiting for moonlight and dawn to meet and wake them into the light of praise of the God, whose rising was heralded by Brother Sun beginning to rise over the crest of Mount Subasio.

All of this is Assisi, and it is still here as I lie within the city walls, three floors up looking out now at first light across the tiled roofs to the dome of St. Mary of the Angels and waiting to hear bells. A single car hums below my window, and I begin a song of dawn, one of the psalms I most love.

> The heavens are telling the glory of God;
>> and the firmament proclaims his handiwork.
> Day to day pours forth speech,
>> and night to night declares knowledge.
> There is no speech, nor are there words;
>> their voice is not heard;
> yet their voice goes out through all the earth,
>> and their words to the end of the world.
>
> In the heavens he has set a tent for the sun,
>> which comes out like a bridegroom from his wedding canopy,
>> and like a strong man runs its course with joy.
> Its rising is from the end of the heavens,
>> and its circuit to the end of them;
>> and nothing is hidden from its heat. (Psalm 19:1–6)

I look up from the words on the page and look out the window and see the sun now igniting the hills across the Valley of Spoleto, and I go to the upper roof garden where Francis's brother, the sun, is just starting its rise over the crest of Mount Subasio, and I am filled with joy and wonder—this is Assisi to me.

Chapter Two

· · ·

THE BLESSING OF ASSISI

As I sit here above the cobblestones that are slowly coming to life in the morning footsteps upon them, as the shop-keepers open their doors and the townspeople start to move about with their day, I think of how being up, off the streets, then as now, was an important status symbol—to be away from the squalor and street dung, the stench of carts that took away lepers or criminals. How might it have sounded and looked in Francis's day with wooden wheels rattling over cobblestones? Most people want to be sheltered from rubbing elbows with that.

The pedestrians of Roman times, the Etruscans, all walked these ancient streets that I am looking across and separated from. Almost all who traveled beneath this roof garden just wanted to get home, go inside to the peace of their own sanctuary. Almost all were seeking to rise above, to be higher, whereas, it was from places such as these that I am moved to contemplate the glaring fact that St. Francis was always seeking the lower ways, the lower, undignified places of the poor.

He was always going down into the earth, this saint, this poor man reborn of the caves, of the depths. Even after ascending the heights of Mount La Verna in Tuscany where he received the wounds of Christ, he descends again here, to this Assisi where now, almost eight hundred years later, he is again below ground level, in his tomb—in the basilica which I see emerging, glistening pink and white as the morning mist rises from around it. There he lies in the crypt of the Lower Basilica dedicated to his name. He is Francis of *Assisi*, and this is the city he blessed with these words:

> Lord, it is believed that in olden days this city was a refuge of evil people. But now it is clear that in your large mercy and at a time of your choosing, you have shown your special superabundant compassion. Through your goodness alone, you have chosen Assisi to be a place of refuge for those who know you in truth, who give glory to your name, and who waft toward all Christian people the perfume of right reputation, holy life, true doctrine, and evangelical perfection. Therefore I pray you, O Lord Jesus Christ, father of mercies, that you not dwell on our ingratitude, but remember always the immense compassion you have shown this city. Let it always be a place of refuge for those who really know you and glorify your blessed name forever.
>
> Amen.[1]

I remember years ago, standing at the spot near the Casa Gualdi on the road to St. Mary of the Angels where Francis blessed his city from his litter as he was carried from the bishop's palace in Assisi to the plain below Assisi. He was making his slow way to the place where he rebuilt the small chapel of Our Lady of the Angels, which he dubbed the Porziuncola, the Little Portion, around which the early brothers lived and next to which Francis died on the barren earth, owning nothing, possessing only the earth that his meekness had inherited.

From where I stood near Casa Gualdi, the site of an ancient leper hospital, I could see Assisi spread out before me. As I took in its panorama, its two great basilicas, one for Francis and one for Clare, held together, like two great stone bookends, I thought of all the stories that are this city, which was smaller at the time of St. Francis and did not include the two great basilicas. It was built on the ruins of the ancient Roman city that preceded it, and by the end of the thirteenth century, the city walls extended some seventy-five-hundred feet around the city, a significant expansion from the Roman city whose wall, according to the Augustan Assisi-born poet, Propertius, was five thousand feet long.

Where I am writing this today years later, here in the Casa Papa Giovanni, the morning mist has turned to a light fog, and Assisi fades in and out of its wisps. It makes me think of the ancient sentries—the protectors of the city—who looked out from the fortifications and how they must have strained and squinted, as I must now in this pale light, to see what lies beyond the walls, to be certain there was no enemy lurking, waiting for an unguarded moment to try to find a way in.

A heavy thud of the huge main door here at Casa Papa Giovanni reminds me that gates could swing shut on mornings such as these, and in my imagination I can identify also with the primal fears of Assisians during the centuries of invasions across these now quiet lands, and how the gate—each simple, single gate—preserved and protected the city. And I am grateful for the gates of Assisi and will remember to thank them the next time I pass through them. They deserve that attention and recognition.

Today eight gates are the way in and out of Assisi: Porta San Giacomo a Muro Rupto, Porta Perlici, Porta Moiano, Porta San Pietro, Porta Sementone, Porta San Francesco, Porta Nuova, and Porta dei Cappuccini, which was previously called Porta San Antonio which, in turn, had replaced the old Porta San Rufino. Most of the present gates date to the fourteenth century or later, and therefore after the death of St. Francis in 1226. But there are four extant gates that were there at the time of St. Francis: Porta San Giacomo a Muro Rupto, Porta San Pietro, Porta Sementone, and Porta Moiano. Porta San Giorgio is no longer extant as a gate—it was the gate of the church and school of San Giorgio during Francis's lifetime and is today simply an arch within the city.

In order to understand the importance of the gates of Assisi in the time of St. Francis, we have to leave the world in which we live and travel back to the thirteenth century, to this small Umbrian city on the side of Mount Subasio in central Italy. It is a walled city punctuated by gates where taxes are collected from merchants and farmers coming to sell their wares in the city.

As the only way in and out of the city, the gate is an essential part of the city's fortifications against the outside world. The citizens know they are only as safe as the city gates are impenetrable. The doors of the stone gates are made of wood, reinforced by thick iron nails, and are locked shut at night. And in addition to these thick wooden doors, the passageways of the major gates are closed with a separate heavy, wooden portcullis, a kind of fail-safe sliding door on the inside of the main door that is made of oak bars with iron bars at the bottom. It can be quickly released and dropped from the barbican above to double-protect the main door; or if the main door has been penetrated, to crush those trying to get in and to buy time for the defenders to regroup before the portcullis itself is penetrated.

The façade of the gate displays shields and escutcheons and other civic emblems and coats of arms relating to whoever is ruling the city: the pope or emperor, for example. There are frescoes, too, or small statues or friezes of the city's patron whom the inhabitants expect to ward off evil from their city. And on the very top is a battlement whose configuration determines whether the city is Guelph or Ghibelline. A Guelph city is a papal city, and a Ghibelline city is imperial. The Ghibelline battlement is swallow-tailed, whereas the Guelph battlement is U-shaped and looks like upside-down teeth. In both cases the defenders place their crossbows, or whatever weapon they are using, into the gaps between the teeth or inside the swallowtail. (One way of remembering which is the loyalty of Guelph or Ghibelline is that the word *Guelph* contains a *u* as does the English word *church*, and is therefore the papal party.)

Many citizens are employed in maintaining the gates, including guards who are both outside and inside the gate, at least one of whom is stationed at the gate throughout the night; there are cashiers, inspectors of merchandise and of people, and masters of the cash box. The manpower surrounding the gates is this impressive because the gate is where the walls, and therefore the city, are most vulnerable.

Many penetrate the gates of Assisi over the centuries, some legally—farmers and merchants and friendly visitors—but others illegally, as conquerors who are not admitted but who break their way through. There are the powerful and the humble, saints and sinners, Etruscans and Romans, Byzantines and Goths, Lombards and Franks at the time of Charlemagne, and conquerors and their soldiers from minor duchies during the so-called "Dark Night" of the years 800 to 1000. There are those who come during the period of wars between Italian city states, and in particular, the squabbles between Assisi and Perugia, its neighboring city. At the time of Francis, Assisi was a Ghibelline city and Perugia a Guelph city; there are feudal lords and peasants, warriors and merchants and clergy; in more modern times the French again, this time under Napoleon, who stables his horses in the Basilica of St. Mary of the Angels; and there are the Fascists and Nazis in the 1940s who occupy the city of Assisi.

How rich, then, is its history, this city on a hill, this city which still holds within its gates the blessing he bestowed upon it, the Little Poor Man, the Mirror of Christ, the quintessential Christian disciple, Francis of *Assisi.*

Chapter Three
· · ·

OF WALLS AND GATES

FROM MY ROOFTOP PERCH INSIDE THE CITY WALLS, ALL OF ASSISI lies before me. There is one single aspect that is most impressive—Assisi is a walled, fortified town. I can follow the undulating outline of the outer walls that separate it from the green valley and the sunflowers and fields of poppies below. As my eye traces the centuries of human stories built into rock and stone, I can see that each wall is pierced with an entrance, a gate.

And gates are more than openings in the city wall. They suggest mystery, these ancient portals that surround this Umbrian hill town. Not just the mystery of St. Francis and St. Clare, but the mystery of the gates themselves, as I soon discovered in trying to find historical information about them. The mystery, too, of the very notion of a gate—is it just a way in and out of a walled city? Or is it something more? Is it a passage that affects us internally? Is it, in fact, symbolic of the passages we make through and into stages or transformations of our lives?

Gates are portals of entry into the places we would inhabit. Tourists use them as passageways rather than passages to a new way of being in a place. There are rituals of entry that are available to those who would learn reverence; for without reverence, place becomes mere scenery.

On the simplest level, gates are holes in the walls of a fortified city. And one thinks of Robert Frost saying, "Something there is that doesn't love a wall," and how he wondered what the walls were intended to wall in or wall out. Always, it seems, there is the "enemy" beyond the walls, which may be of our own making, who wants to sneak in and take over our city, appropriating as his or her own the property and goods and people within. And those of us within know and fear this threat to our lives and, in turn, wall ourselves in for protection, even though the "enemy" may already be inside our walls, may in fact reside within our own walled-in hearts.

At the time of St. Francis the enemy was very much inside and outside the walls of the city. Pope and emperor were both vying for Assisi and its outlying properties. Perugia, its natural enemy, was on the other side of the Tiber River about fifteen miles away. In ancient times, Perugia was inhabited by the Etruscans, and Assisi was inhabited by Umbrians: two peoples one on each side of the dividing Tiber River. In Francis's time Perugia, as mentioned earlier, was a papal city, while Assisi was, for a time in Francis's youth, an imperial city with the emperor's viceroy installed in the Rocca Maggiore, the fortress castle that towered over the city.

And within the city of Assisi itself there were minor and major quarrels and feuds between the nobles and the rising merchant class, and families themselves seemed always be quarreling over one thing or another. Francis himself was but a youth when the merchants of Assisi revolted against the nobles and the imperial fortress, tearing down the Rocca Maggiore and using its stones to expand and strengthen the city walls.

It is no wonder that St. Francis once had this exchange with the Bishop of Assisi who said to St. Francis, "I think your life is too hard, too rough. You don't possess anything in this world." "My Lord," Francis responded, "If we had possessions, we would need weapons to defend them."[2]

No wonder, too, that St. Francis forbade his brothers to have dwellings of their own and to appropriate nothing for themselves. Everything was to be considered on loan from God, the Great Almsgiver; and the brothers were to treat all created things, animate and inanimate, as good gifts of God that are made evil by our own greed and possessiveness. It is not any individual thing in itself that is evil, but our appropriation of it as our own without reference to the God who created it, who keeps it in existence, and who sanctifies it. For St. Francis all things are to be treated with reverence and with reference to their Creator; through them we are to offer God praise and thanksgiving.

When one enters or leaves Assisi today, there are no locked gates. No gates are manned with guards who regulate and tax those entering the city. There are instead policewomen and policemen at Porta Nuova, the New Gate, who direct cars to the streets that are open to automobile traffic, or who point out what streets are one-way or perhaps closed temporarily on given occasions. So, by and large, the eight gates of the city are simply ways in and out of the city and reminders of what once was when a walled Umbrian hill town was a world unto itself with its own government and lifestyle, its own proud independence.

But even today, with all its gates open to the public, there is something special about Assisi, something that transcends its historical past. The pilgrim, and even the serious traveler, is aware of an intangible peace that begins to settle in the soul—I know it did in mine. And as an English teacher of many years and a lover of great stories, I was thrilled to discover that even so inveterate a traveler and observer and teller of tales as the novelist Henry James felt the difference Assisi is:

> The city wall…straggles up the steep green hill and meets the crumbling skeleton of the fortress. On the side off from the town the mountain plunges into a deep ravine, the opposite face of which is formed by the powerful undraped shoulder of Monte Subasio, a fierce reflector of the sun. Gorge and mountain are wild enough, but their frown expires in the teeming softness of the great vale of Umbria. To lie aloft there on the grass with silver-grey ramparts at one's back and the warm rushing wind in one's ears, and watch the beautiful plain mellow into the tones of twilight, was as exquisite a form of repose as ever fell to a tired tourist's lot.[3]

Perhaps that is why I am moved to pray these words from Psalm 118 each time I return to Assisi and pass through any of its gates into the sanctuary this city has become for me:

> Open to me the gates of righteousness,
> that I may enter through them
> and give thanks to the Lord.
> This is the gate of the Lord;
> the righteous shall enter through it. (Psalm 118:19–20)

Thus, the title of this book, *Enter Assisi*. It is both an invitation to the reader to enter Assisi, but it is also a sort of stage direction to Assisi itself, a cue, a prayerful request of Assisi to enter our lives and to show us what it is that brings such Jamesian repose to us who enter; and to show us, too, how we are to meditate on that intangible repose until we see and understand that this repose is a God-given peace we are meant to take with us when we exit Assisi's gates and return again to the roads of our lives.

Chapter Four

. . .

ENTER ASSISI

SITTING HERE THIS MORNING, WITH MY CAPPUCCINO, I LOOK west and I can see in the distance, about two and a half miles and a short bus ride away, the basilica and town of St. Mary of the Angels. I see in that short distance, the space of half a lifetime that has passed; for it was there, forty years ago, that I, like many others over the years, first exited the train station at St. Mary of the Angels and saw the distant medieval hill town of Assisi, its pink and yellow stone spread across natural terraces on a spur of Mount Subasio. On each end of the city are the two grand churches that you presume are the Basilica of St. Francis and the Basilica of St. Clare, holding all of that stone library in place.

Stone: Stone houses, stone walls, stone gates; you hear echoes of Christ's words to St. Francis, "Go, and repair my house which, as you see, is falling into ruins." And the young Francis then began to beg stones to repair the small chapel of San Damiano, which lay beyond the gates of the stone city he had grown up in. Echoes, too, of Pope Innocent III's dream of Rome's Basilica of St. John Lateran, the pope's own church as bishop of Rome, beginning to collapse and Francis shouldering one of the stone arches to keep the church from falling down.

Stone churches, stone foundations for God; wattle huts for Francis and the brothers where they lived on the plain below Assisi, the plain you are standing on now as you lift your eyes to Assisi on the distant hillside.

You are quite near the Porziuncola, another small chapel Francis repaired with his own hands. Porziuncola—"the Little Portion"—the chapel on the same plain where lepers and other marginal people lived, the poor and meek who, as Jesus said, will inherit the earth. The Porziuncola, which today is housed inside another grand basilica: the Basilica of St. Mary of the Angels.

Francis left the beautiful city in the distance to descend to where you stand wanting to leave and ascend to the mountain town where he lies buried under stones of stone. You want to be near his bones that rest in a stone sarcophagus beneath two churches: the Romanesque Lower Basilica and the Gothic Upper Basilica. You realize you're going to have to sort out all that stone before you understand the man who gathered and worked with stones for God and who rejected anything as solid as stone for his own temporary dwellings on this earth.

You will need to pass in and out of the eight important gates of the city to understand anything of the passages of Francis's life— and your own. How, for example, the spirit is as grounded as stone, the body is as airy as everything you let go of.

And so you lift your luggage onto the waiting bus and head for the stone city with the stone gates you'll enter; and exit, when you finally do, a changed person like St. Francis and St. Clare before you.

We ourselves are the gate we must pass through, as I learned the very first time I passed through the arch of St. Clare that leads into her piazza. I had come to learn, to write, to discover the mysteries of this lovely city I'd dreamed of as a boy.

Standing alone late at night, suitcase in hand, in the spring of 1972, having made the bus trip up the hill from the train station,

I looked up from the Piazza of St. Clare to the steep stone stairs that led to the Via Galeazzo Alessi, the street above St. Clare's Piazza, the street where at No. 10 the Franciscan Sisters of the Atonement had their *pensione*, St. Anthony's Hospice. Though it is now called, "St. Anthony's Guest House," I love the word *hospice*, which conjures up the Middle Ages and medieval pilgrimages and the feel of a place of healing and rest. That is what "St. Anthony's Hospice" became for me. I learned there that I myself was the gate I had to pass through as I went in and out of the gates of Assisi. My own inner, locked gates had to open to God's knocking.

Now, writing this years later in Assisi as a gentle rain falls onto the tile roofs of the buildings below and across from my window, I remember how I found a healing peace in something so simple as the spring rains that fell on the cobblestone streets of Assisi and on the stone stairs outside my window that made mini-waterfalls of the rushing water. And afterward the rain would hang on in small droplets clinging in a row on the tiny balcony outside the room where I wrote, lost in the words, unaware, until I looked up, that the rain was still there in the drops that surprised me as they tenaciously clung to the iron railings of the balcony.

The rain itself became a gate into the words and into the place of peace within me. I remember that spring in Assisi as rain and the rain was the gate that led me into my own center.

Every day, when the rain was over and the writing for the day was set aside, I'd walk down the long stone steps to the Piazza of St. Clare and from there walk through the arch of the ancient church of San Giorgio into the Piazza del Comune, the city's main piazza, and wait for the noon bells to ring and the pigeons to swoop down into the piazza for their own *pranzo,* their little noonday lunch. And after that midday celebration of the birds, I'd walk back on the middle road from the piazza that led directly to the *pensione* for *pranzo*, which was at 1 P.M., followed by a *riposo*, nap, followed by roaming the streets of Assisi, trying to get the feel of the city for my first book which became *Francis: The Journey and the Dream.*

Chapter Five
. . .

THROUGH THE WRITER'S GATE

I FIRST ENTERED ASSISI'S GATES TO FIND WORDS, AND EVERY leaving and returning found more words until the words themselves became the passage in and the passage out of Assisi. And *Francis: The Journey and the Dream* was the first gift of words that Assisi gave me: my first book whose symbolic gate is that of opening up words on the page that open up something of who St. Francis was.

It was not my idea to write a book on St. Francis. It was the idea of Fr. Jeremy Harrington, who was at that time editor of *St. Anthony Messenger* magazine, a popular Catholic magazine with a large and broad circulation. He requested of my provincial minister, Fr. Roger Huser, that I be sent to Assisi to write a book about St. Francis. It was to be a popular book, "popular" in the sense that it wasn't intended to be a scholarly work, but a work for the ordinary people who read *St. Anthony Messenger*. In addition, Fr. Jeremy asked me to write a book that would be released in conjunction with the Franco Zeffirelli film, *Brother Sun, Sister Moon*, which was then in production—and, in fact, the English version of the film did come out almost at the same time as the book.

The Italian version of the film was released while I was still in Assisi writing, and through a series of misunderstandings and mixed messages, I ended up attending the premier at the

Teatro Metastasio in Assisi, even though attendance was by invitation only. I wrongly presumed that my Franciscan habit was my ticket and was, in fact, admitted without any questions, the usher presuming I must be some important American Franciscan from the Franciscan Curia in Rome; nothing, of course, could have been further from the truth.

But I did see the premier and spoke with Franco Zeffirelli afterward. He asked me to take the man who played Francis, Graham Faulkner, out back to rescue him from the "adoration" of the fans. He was painfully shy and almost ran outside with me.

At the time I wrote the book, I was an English teacher and one of the spiritual directors at St. Francis High School Seminary in Cincinnati; and my teaching and listening to the seminarians and my concern for them, made them, in one sense, my principal audience. I knew what their dreams were, how St. Francis had inspired them to want to be Franciscans, and how they longed for a meaning and purpose in their lives that was more than just a result of the culture of the early 1970s. All of these factors influenced the kind of book *Francis: The Journey and the Dream* turned out to be.

As with all authors, there was my own story as well, my own journey with St. Francis. It began when, at the age of thirteen, I pulled a life of St. Francis from the shelf of our school library at Gallup, New Mexico's junior high school. It was entitled *God's Troubadour, the Story of St. Francis of Assisi* and was written by Sophie Jewett in 1910. Years later I used to scour libraries, looking for that first book I'd read about St. Francis, but I couldn't find it because I couldn't remember the author or the title, although I knew I would recognize the book if I ever saw it again. Then, in 2000, I found it in the young adult section of the public library in Milbrook, New York, where I was researching another writing project. When I opened up the book again those many years later, I could see why Sophie Jewett's book had touched me so. It was beautifully written, with simple Franciscan sentences, simple rhythms, and a mysterious opening paragraph that caught my attention immediately. It goes like this:

> Under the arched gate of a city wall, a group of people stood watching the road that wound down the mountain and off across the plain. The road lay dusty and white in September sunshine, and the eyes of the watchers followed it easily until it hid itself in a vast forest that filled half of the valley. On the point where road and forest met, the sharpest eyes were fixed. Assisi, at whose gate the watchers stood, lies far across the sea in beautiful Italy. It is a little city, built on a mountainside, with a great wall all about it, and a castle on the height above, and it looks very much as it did on that September afternoon more than seven hundred years ago, when Francis Bernardone waited for his father.[4]

When I read the above paragraph, I was hooked and couldn't put the book down and ended up wanting to be a follower of St. Francis. I wanted someday to stand under that same arched gate in Assisi and see St. Francis there waiting for his father.

Many other books about St. Francis followed that first book, including, when I was a student at St. Francis High School seminary, Fr. Isidore O'Brien's *Life of St. Francis*, Felix Timmermans's

The Perfect Joy of St. Francis, G.K. Chesterton's book-length essay on St. Francis, and the monumental life of St. Francis by Johannes Jorgensen.

Every year when I'm in Assisi and am walking back streets to the Cathedral of San Rufino, I pause along the way and look up a long flight of stairs to a house at the very top, to a plaque honoring Johannes Jorgensen who lived in that house for over thirty years. He was known in Assisi as "the man in white" because he always wore a white suit when he went out in public.

Here are a few brief paragraphs from *Report to Greco*, an autobiographical novel by Nikos Kazantzakis, the Greek poet, who also wrote a novel about St. Francis. He is talking here of how, as a young man, he encountered Johannes Jorgensen in Assisi. Here is a part of how Kazantzakis reconstructs his meeting with Johannes Jorgensen:

> [Jorgensen] asked me, "Why do you love St. Francis?"…
>
> "I love him for two reasons," I replied. "First, because he is a poet, one of the greatest of the pre-Renaissance. Bending over even the most insignificant of God's creatures, he heard the mortal element they have inside them: melody."
>
> "And second?" asked Jorgensen.
>
> "Second, I love him because by means of love and ascetic discipline his soul conquered reality—hunger, cold, disease, scorn, injustice, ugliness (what men without wings call reality)—and succeeded in transubstantiating this reality into a joyous, palpable dream truer than truth itself. He discovered the secret so sought after by medieval alchemists: how to transubstantiate

even the basest metal into pure gold…. [Through] the miracle of mystical alchemy, he subdued reality, delivered mankind from necessity, and inwardly transformed all his flesh into spirit…."

And Jorgensen responded, "That is not enough…. That is why your face appears so worried…. You are still struggling, you have not achieved deliverance, and this struggle day after day is exhausting you. This is the reason I stopped you this morning and spoke to you."

Then there's an argument that ends up with Jorgensen telling Kazantzakis of his own struggles, of his conversion which began when he fell on his knees in the chapel of the Porziuncola when he was a young man searching and without faith. Then Kazantzakis asks Jorgensen, "How did deliverance come to you?" And Jorgensen responds,

Calmly and without noise, as it most always does. Just as a fruit ripens and grows sweetly succulent, so my heart ripened and became sweetly succulent. Suddenly everything seemed simple and certain to me. The agonies, hesitations, and battles all ceased. I sat at Francis's feet and entered heaven. Francis, Francis himself, is the Brother Gatekeeper who opened the door for me.[5]

These books, and others, were my gates into St. Francis and his city. They all in some way formed the kind of book I would one day write about St. Francis. We're formed, after all, not only by our experiences, but also by the kinds of books we read, the movies we see, and the music we listen to. In other words, writers write out of who they are, what they know, and their own particular way of seeing the world around them and within them.

When my classmates and I left the high school seminary and moved on to our novitiate, we studied Fr. Cuthbert's *Life of Francis* under the guidance of our saintly novice master, Fr. Benno Heidlage. Then followed our temporary profession of vows and our college years at Duns Scotus College in Detroit where our cleric master, Fr. Mel Brady, taught us early Franciscan sources from the mimeographed notes of his brother, the esteemed Franciscan scholar Fr. Ignatius Brady. This material was especially valuable in my own Franciscan formation and was essential background material for what I was to write in *Francis: The Journey and the Dream*. All of these factors I mention only to show how a book doesn't come out of a vacuum; it comes out of a person who has a formative past out of which the book emerges.

But, in the end, when it comes to writing about a human life, no matter how much research or lack thereof is involved, what matters is the story itself—the narrative arc—and how well the story is told. With all the naiveté of my comparative youth—I was thirty-five years old when I wrote *Francis: The Journey and the Dream*—I somehow opted for telling St. Francis's story from within—a story interior to Francis, though written in the third-person point of view. Whatever was I thinking? How could I have known Francis's thoughts? But try as I might otherwise, that is the writing voice and the point of view that kept coming to me. So, in the end I went with it, let it happen, and the words kept filling the pages day after day as I sat at my little desk in Room 12 at St. Anthony Guest House in Assisi. The voice and words kept falling onto the page in a kind of rush, and Francis grew in my mind and on the page as a full-fledged character. And when he finally died, I knew that something had happened, if not in the pages of the book, then in me. Something was there on the page and in me that wasn't there before. A book had happened.

I had no idea whether or not the book had any merit or relevance for others, but I felt emptied and filled simultaneously; and I felt that something had been created that had changed me in the process. That is, I believe, every writer's experience at some point. You also realize that your character has outgrown and gone further and in different directions than your initial intention. The writing has become the gate into your own Narnia, in my case, the gate into the Assisi I had dreamed of as a boy.

One cannot, of course, enter into the mind and heart of another, let alone of a medieval man who died in 1226—without the power of the imagination. I stumble to express this reality, so I turn to the poet John Keats and what he said in a letter dated November 1817: "I am certain of nothing but the holiness of the Heart's affections and the truth of the Imagination—What the imagination seizes as Beauty must be truth—whether it existed before or not."[6]

That's an extraordinary claim for the imagination, but when I was writing *Francis: The Journey and the Dream*, there was for me some truth to what Keats said. I felt that what I was writing was somehow true, as true as the historical facts upon which the story was based. I was using as my outline a small life of St. Francis by the Franciscan scholar and biographer of St. Clare, Nesta de Robeck, and I had, as well, what I remembered of the basic content of the biographies I had read of St. Francis to that date. And, of course, I had my experience as a Franciscan friar to help me tell St. Francis's story for a modern popular audience. And what I kept feeling was that the St. Francis in the pages of the book rang true to me, whether or not the story was the exact historical reality of the St. Francis who lived outside the pages of the book. It was, after all, not a biography, but a personal poetic meditation on a man whose life and writings I had tried to follow for almost twenty years prior to writing the book.

I felt at times that St. Francis was more my muse than a detached subject. And many readers must have felt something similar about the book for it to have continued to endure, these forty some years, as a sort of introduction to the life of St. Francis. Many, too, as I hoped they would, moved on from this first story to study the writings and original sources of the life and times of St. Francis. Perhaps that's what a popular book does: it inspires the reader to learn more, to see what original sources are available, to maybe even begin to see St. Francis as their own personal model of how to walk in the footsteps of the Poor Christ, the Christ whose first words to us were, "Blessed are the poor of spirit, for theirs is the kingdom of heaven."

The longer I try to live the Franciscan rule and life, the more convinced I am that the poverty of St. Francis's embrace of the leper, of what is at first repulsive but then turns into sweetness of soul and body, is at the core of St. Francis's meaning for us today. It is a poverty and a love that began in him as a response to the poverty and love of Jesus Christ who, as St. Paul writes, is the one who

> though he was in the form of God,
>   did not regard equality with God
>   as something to be exploited,

but emptied himself,
   taking the form of a slave,
   being born in human likeness
And being found in human form,
   He humbled himself
   And became obedient to the point of death—
   even death on a cross" (Philippians 2:6–8).

That's the real story behind the story of who St. Francis was and what he did. And that is what I tried to flesh out for popular readers in *Francis: The Journey and the Dream,* written in Assisi where, under an arched gate, the young Francis is still waiting for his father.

Chapter Six

· · ·

STAGES

THEN THE RAINS WOULD COME, AND THE PINK ASSISI STONE would shine with light though dark clouds were pressing down on the city. That light was what I experienced the first weeks I lived in Assisi in 1972, and the rain washing down the cobblestone streets much as it had when the young Francis sloshed and slipped down them, the rivulets of rain becoming rushing streams that washed clean the waste and sewer-soaked streets.

And now as heavy rainclouds settle over Assisi this late September morning, and the whole city seems enveloped in a huge cloud, and I know the rain will come, I suddenly see what I've guessed at intermittently over the years: Assisi is a living prayer. Its narrow streets stream with pilgrims year after year, their hearts filled with hope that maybe here in this place their prayers will be answered. They ask St. Francis and St. Clare to intercede for them, to help them know what it is they are looking for. They cross the threshold of the Basilica of St. Clare and kneel before the San Damiano crucifix that gave St. Francis the direction for his life: "Go and repair my house which, as you see, is falling into ruin." They pray before the same crucifix the prayer of St. Francis:

> Most High, Glorious God,
> enlighten the darkness of my heart,
> and give me correct faith

sure hope and perfect charity,

with understanding and knowledge, Lord,

so that I may fulfill your holy and true command.

Amen.[7]

How many years of days have I sat at this second floor window watching the rain lessen and the clouds lift slowly and the sun begin to break through! There's a certain light that is there in all three stages of the lightening that I have seen in its various transformations all day long. They symbolize for me the three prayers contained in the prayer of Francis before the crucifix: (1) Enlighten the darkness of my heart; (2) give me a right faith, a certain hope and a perfect love, with understanding and knowledge; (3) that I may carry out your holy and true command.

These are the stages of conversion: darkness of heart to faith's illumination of knowledge and understanding to the light of the will living in God's will. And that is what I believe every pilgrim seeks, no matter what he or she thinks they really want. It is a conversion simply though subtly wrought, as in "The Light Continues" by Linda Gregg:

Every evening, an hour before
the sun goes down, I walk toward
its light, wanting to be altered.
Always in quiet, the air still.
...
When I return, the moon is there.
Like a changing of the guard.
I don't expect the light
to save me, but I do believe

in the ritual. I believe
I am being born a second time
in this very plain way.[8]

That is very simply what a pilgrim does: walk. And it is the
way the pilgrim prays, with his or her feet. And the feet walk
through dark clouds to illumination to the light that is holy
action. Through dark, cloud-filled days to a hint of subtle lightening to the sun breaking through, the feet taking us where we
least thought we'd go, where before we had thought darkness
dwelt, and finding there instead, in bright sunlight, the broken,
the poor, the marginal, those made ugly or disfigured by abuse
and oppression and woundedness. We are changed simply by
walking, rain or shine, toward and back from whatever shrine
we had thought contained our hope and longing. We walk back
toward what was there all along that we could not see. And what
was it we could not see? And what is the portal's meaning that
takes us there? The poet Rainer Maria Rilke puts it this way in
"The Portal":

So much distance is meant by it:
just as with the backdrop of a scene
the world is meant; and as through that scene
the hero strides, cloaked in his action's mantle: —

so the darkness of this doorway strides acting
onto the tragic theater of its depths,
as boundless and seething as God the Father
and just as He transforming wondrously
into a Son, who is distributed here

among many small, almost unspeaking roles,
all taken from misery's repertoire.

For it's only (this we know) from
the blind, the cast-out, and the mad
that, like a great actor, the Saviour emerges.[9]

Chapter Seven

• • •

PASSING THROUGH THE GATE

THERE IS SOMETHING ABOUT PASSING THROUGH A GATE THAT marks subjective time.

The first time, for example, that I passed through the Porta Nuova, the main gate into the center of the city, marked the beginning of my life as a serious writer—serious in the sense that I passed through the Porta Nuova with a contract in hand. I had come to this mystical city to write a book about St. Francis. Three months later I left through that same gate a changed man from the one who had entered through that gate not knowing what that passage signified.

It is called the Porta Nuova, the New Gate, because it is the most recent of the gates built after the time of St. Francis. The Porta Nuova is one of a ring of gates that circle inner ancient gates that predate the Middle Ages and today are represented by arches within the city itself. The recent gates form the outer ring one must pass through, as into the narthex of a cathedral, that prepares the soul to pass through the inner gates into the sacred space of the city's medieval sanctuary, the Piazza del Comune, the main piazza of the commune of Assisi.

I call the Piazza del Comune the city's medieval sanctuary because it locates the most important space of this medieval city, the space that marks out the transition from a city once ruled by foreign nobility, either of the German nobility or the papacy, to a commune ruled by its own representatives. In 1210 a treaty was struck between the local nobility and the citizens of Assisi whereby all the citizens of the town were enfranchised, freed from obligations to a master or Lord, and incorporated into the protective collective order of the commune of the city which had been formed by the sworn association of the city's free men. And between 1212 and 1215 the communal palace was built in the Piazza del Comune.

Assisi had become an independent city-state. And even today there is that fierce independence of the inhabitants of Assisi. They are proud of their city, of its heritage, of the saint who made them famous beyond the walls that have encircled them for hundreds of years and have protected the center of the city, the Piazza del Comune, despite the two grand basilicas at each end of the city which, during the lifetimes of Francis and Clare, lay outside the city walls: the Basilica of St. Francis and the Basilica of St. Clare.

It is fitting that these two great saints of Assisi were buried outside the original city gates. They walked out of the city, a passage through a gate that symbolized their rejection of the commercial values that dominated their city. They "left the world," meaning the values of the city of their birth, to begin the new life that God had shown them among the poor and the rejected who lived beyond the protection of the city walls, those who lived on the margins of the society that Assisi represented.

Today when you pass through the New Gate, Porta Nuova, on your way into the city, you travel along a wide street, the Via Borgo Aretino, that takes you to the medieval arch between the Basilica of St. Clare and the city, and through which you pass into the Piazza of St. Clare in front of the basilica where St. Clare lies buried in the crypt. Then, moving through the Piazza of St. Clare, you pass through an arch that goes back to the time of the youth of Francis and Clare and which brings you, after a short walk, into the Piazza del Comune. The pilgrim finds this way of entering the city a significant passage because one has to pass through the reality of the noble Lady Clare in order to grasp the meaning of the Piazza del Comune, the piazza of the common people.

The childhood home of St. Francis is just below the Piazza del Comune because his father was a merchant, and the merchants lived in the area of that piazza. Clare herself lived above the Piazza del Comune right next to the Piazza of San Rufino, the cathedral piazza. Her family, the Offreduccio family, was of the nobility whose feudal ascendancy at one time dominated those who lived in the lower parts of the city.

Clare herself, when she left home to join St. Francis and the brothers who were living at the Porziuncola on the plain below Assisi, walked from her home in the area of the nobles down into and across the Piazza del Comune, where Francis had lived as a boy, and further down yet to the area of the old Cathedral of St. Mary Major and out through the Porta Moiano, the most important gate of her life. For through that gate she walked into a whole new way of living, apart from her family, apart from her status as a beautiful young noble woman, a way of living as a poor lady among the poor.

Francis himself walked out of Assisi from the old Cathedral of St. Mary Major, through the lower gate of San Giacomo onto the road that led to Gubbio, a neighboring town where he knew a rich man, Federico Spadalunga (Frederick Long-Sword), who, one tradition claims, had fought with Francis in the war against Perugia. There was, in fact, a long tradition of friendship and military alliance between Assisi and Gubbio; and Gubbio, too, had been ignominiously defeated in battle by Perugia.

It is thought that the Spadalunga family were cloth merchants, as was the family of St. Francis. Perhaps they knew one another from that connection as well; perhaps, too, Francis and Federico had been imprisoned together in Perugia. But the latter is speculation. It is an interesting speculation; but much of why Francis went to Gubbio and who the Spadalungas were to him remains cloaked in the mystery of time past, through whose gate it is sometimes impossible to pass.

In fact, much of the history of medieval towns like Assisi and Gubbio remains impenetrable because of the destruction of documents and monuments due to wars and fires and the plague and other vicissitudes of ancient cities. But that is a part of their allure, part of the joy of continuing research and speculation, part of the joy of discovering, the joy of a possible epiphany, a sudden realization of why and how things happened beyond the wardrobe of time present.

Chapter Eight
· · ·

YOUR OWN PORTA SAN GIACOMO
A MURO RUPTO

ACCORDING TO THE GREAT FRANCISCAN SCHOLAR ARNALDO
Fortini, after Francis had renounced his patrimony in the bishop's courtyard, he left through Porta San Giacomo a Muro
Rupto, the Gate of St. James of the Breached Wall, as through
a reverse breaching of the wall that would free him from Assisi's
commercial and military values. He left, having stripped naked,
a poor man completely dependent on God.

But what is it that makes one truly poor? And what is the
poverty of St. Francis that I have reached for all my life? Through
all the books I have written, I have tried to define for myself
and others why St. Francis was poor and why we would want to
follow him in that poverty.

In one sense the poverty of St. Francis is a mystery because
only he can know what it meant to him, and no human being is
wholly fathomable. What we do know, however, is what Francis
himself said about poverty.

First and foremost, for Francis poverty is Gospel poverty, the
poverty of Jesus Christ, "who though he was in the form of God,
did not count equality with God something to be grasped, but
emptied himself…" (Philippians 2:6–7).

This *kenosis,* or self-emptying of Christ, *is* Franciscan poverty.
Jesus had to hand over divinity in order to know dependence on

the Father. Francis had to hand over his possessions, and more important, possessiveness itself, in order to know dependence on the same Father.

Not only did Francis experience the pain of his own self-exile from his patrimony, but he went further and exiled himself even to the very borders of his chosen society-in-exile: He went to live among the lepers who lived outside of Assisi. He was no longer a citizen of Assisi. But neither was he a leper. To the citizens of both societies he was the one on the margins, the prophet, a sign, just as Jesus was a sign in his humanity. Jesus was God and not God, a man and not a man, when he came among us. He was a sign of contradiction, just as Francis was when he set out to follow in the footsteps of Jesus.

Francis's giving up of material things was only a sign of that deeper self-emptying. But it is even more than self-emptying. Having an abundance of things gives one the illusion of independence—illusion, because we are all interdependent and dependent on God, who made us, saved us, and sanctifies us. The security that material possessions give us makes even the thought of God something we have to be reminded of, whereas, if we are poor, it is easier to turn to God in praise and thanksgiving for even the smallest gift.

St. Francis believed that everything we have is a gift of God, the Great Almsgiver. We, then, are foolish to be possessive, for nothing is ours; it is only graciously lent to us by God's beneficence. And to bring this home to us as graphically as possible, God's very Son emptied himself of divinity and came among us as one of us, dependent on the Father in life and in death.

Dependence on God through self-emptying—that is the Gospel poverty that St. Francis lived by walking in the footsteps of Jesus; and it all began when the young Francis stripped himself of his clothes and laid them and his patrimony at the feet of his father, Pietro Bernardone. To divest is to become naked before God. It is becoming, in the words of St. Bonaventure, *"Nudus nudum Christum sequi,"* naked to follow the naked Christ.

Nothing makes us feel more vulnerable than to stand naked before others, stripped of our privacy or protective clothing— the indignity of it all! Why, then, would Francis enact such a humiliating gesture if not because he wanted to follow Christ in all things? And why would he want to follow Christ if he did not love him and see in him the very image of the Godhead, which is eternal giving among three Divine Persons?

The Trinity equally generates and loves among themselves and reaches beyond their own inner life to create a universe beyond themselves. They are three Persons made one for us in Jesus Christ, the Incarnation of the Holy Trinity.

The way to this Trinity is the way the Trinity came to us—by descending and disguising their divinity in sending the Second Person to be one of us in order to lead us into their Trinitarian life. This they did that we might be like Christ; and if we do so, we are then drawn by and to the Father through the Spirit of Christ, who is the Holy Spirit.

This is the mystery and secret of life. And it began for Francis when he laid his clothes at the feet of his father and said, "I will no longer say, 'father Pietro Bernardone,' but, 'Our Father who art in heaven.'"

What, then, is the gesture we have to make to begin our total dependence on God? What do we have to surrender to God? What is the nakedness we need to feel to be like Christ Jesus?

But whoa! This is sounding like really heady and heroic stuff. Does this mean we all have to be heroes like St. Francis? Or do we only have to love and serve God with the measure that has been given us to serve and love? We follow in the footsteps of Christ as who *we* are. Though we know all the elements of that following, it is really something quite personal in how we follow in the footsteps of Jesus. As St. Francis himself said at the end of his life, "I have done what was mine to do; may Christ teach you what is yours to do."[10]

What is God showing you that you are to do with your life? However small or great that is, it must be yours and not someone else's. What a stripping, for example, is sickness or aging, or the loss of loved ones, or ultimately the stripping that is the embrace of Sister Death. The important thing is to give humbly and honestly of what God asks you to give. In the end you are the gift God wants; in the meantime each person struggles to know what God wants and whether or not one is really giving the gift of one's self to God. Everyone finds her or his own Porta San Giacomo, the passage through which is the way out of the confining city that keeps one imprisoned in values and mores that make living wholeheartedly in God impossible.

Part Two

DISCOVERING CLARE

Chapter Nine

PORTA MOIANO:
CLARE'S PASSAGE TO A NEW LIFE

In Roman times, where the Bishop's palace stood in
Clare's time, and still stands today, was the old temple
of the god Janus, the god with two faces, one looking
towards the past and the other towards the future. Janus
was the god of beginnings, transitions and changes,
and therefore the god who watched over doorways
and gateways. In the old Roman wall of the Bishop's
garden is, even today, a gateway with the inscription:
post quartum prequartianem, meaning that the devotee
had to invoke the god's help four times, and after the
fourth *precautionem* or prayer, they could then open the
gate into the temple.[11]

THE PORTA MOIANO, THE MOIANO GATE, ABUTS THE WALL THAT
encloses the old cathedral of Santa Maria Maggiore and the bishop's residence, as it did when Francis and Clare lived in Assisi.

Clare was a daughter of the knight Favarone and his wife
Ortolana and therefore, Clare was of the nobility. Her mother
was, in fact, noble in her own right, a descendent of Charlemagne,
and a woman of substance and sense of devotion and adventure
who had made the three great pilgrimages of the Middle Ages:
the Deus (God) Pilgrimage to Jerusalem, the Homo (Human)
Pilgrimage to Rome, and the Angelus (Angel) Pilgrimage to

Monte Gargano south of Rome to the Shrine of St. Michael the Archangel.

Not much is known of Clare's father, and the feudal leader of the family seems to have been her uncle Monaldo who led the attempts to retrieve Clare and later her sister Catherine when they fled the family home to follow Francis and his religious fraternity of Lesser Brothers.

It was through the Moiano Gate that Clare passed from Assisi and its mercantile values to that other world outside the city gates. When one stands inside this gate today, it is not hard to imagine how radical was Clare's passage through the dark night toward what she believed was the light she'd longed for all her life. The light that Francis preached, the light who was Christ, the light that was to be found among the poor and rejected.

Hers had been the life of a much-loved and protected elder daughter who, because of her beauty—she was fair skinned with long blond hair and blue eyes—and her substantial dowry, was expected to marry up and thereby increase the prestige and wealth of the family.

All of which is difficult to imagine these eight hundred years later and even more difficult to research, given the relatively limited resources that remain from thirteenth-century Assisi. How much easier it would be had Clare and Francis lived in the "visitable past" Henry James wrote about—a past near enough to revisit, at least in the mind, the people and places and mores—a past, for example, like the past that I remember over forty years ago when I first lived in Assisi in 1972.

It was a time when one still saw white oxen in the fields, when there were telephone tokens called *gettoni* that you'd buy in a tobacco shop, originally licensed to sell tobacco and salt. It was a time when it was almost impossible to make an international call using the antiquated Italian phone system, now circumvented by the omnipresent *cellulari* (cell phones).

In Rome, for example, to make an international call one would go to the Piazza San Sylvestro and hand your foreign phone number to an operator who would make the call for you and then indicate, by means of a flashing red light above its door, which booth you were to enter to lift the phone there from its cradle—and so often you'd exit soon after because the phone number happened to be busy!

It was a time, too, when a weekly warm bath in Assisi felt luxurious after a week of cold sponge baths. It all seemed so glorious and ancient-feeling when one was young and living in Assisi and in love with St. Francis.

Of St. Clare I knew very little, except for the lovely biography by Nesta de Robeck. Nor did I read Italian, and Latin I could read but with difficulty. St. Anthony's Hospice did have a copy or two of de Robeck's biography. Then one day Sr. Rosita, one of the Franciscan Atonement Sisters there, told me, much to my surprise, that Nesta de Robeck was still alive and resided in an apartment just outside the arch of St. Clare's basilica on Via Borgo Aretino.

My breath caught at the mere mention of someone I thought was surely in heaven! Instead, it seemed, I was the one in paradise, and my Dante-like "Beatrice" was there just down the steps and through the gate a few paces away.

Nesta de Robeck—the Franciscan historian and author of the first good English-language life of St. Clare. Nesta de

Robeck—the famous Secular Franciscan, or as we said in those days, Third Order Franciscan. I didn't know it when I first met Nesta, but she was a friend and confidante of Iris Origo, Marchesa of Val d'Orcia, herself a fine writer and author of *The Merchant of Prado* and *The World of San Bernardino*. Origo's diaries of World War II, *War in Val d'Orcia*, would later be an important influence on my own writing—an inspiration and a how-to text for writing this very chapter.

My first contact with Nesta was through Sr. Rosita who arranged a time when "the Signora would be available." It was all very proper, very English, and full of promise. And this first visit exceeded my expectations. It is engraved in my memory, and I return to it often to feel again the surprise and delight of encountering such an extraordinary woman.

She was quite elderly at the time and was being cared for by a younger Italian woman who had become both companion and caretaker. It was the latter who answered the door the first time I visited and who ushered me up to the second-floor apartment the two shared.

When we entered the apartment, I was surprised to see the exquisite furniture that punctuated the small sitting room. It reminded me of Louis XV furniture in its delicacy and taste, and perhaps it was. And sitting on the couch across the room was a petite, elderly woman, so small she looked like a squashed Victorian lady's hat. She was smiling brightly, her beautiful lavender-blue eyes young and inquisitive.

"Oh, Father, how splendid of you to come," rang out in a distinctive, perfectly articulated Oxford accent from where she sat on a small loveseat.

"Do sit down. This young woman and I are just discussing the sexuality in the novels of D.H. Lawrence. Could you help us?"

I thought I could—and did—sort of, because it was evident that Nesta knew much more than I did and, I suspected, probably had known D.H. Lawrence personally at one time or another. And here I was, an American with a master's degree in English, teaching in a high school seminary; a celibate who was neither an expert on sex nor on D.H. Lawrence, whom I knew mainly from the movie, *Women in Love*, and, at that time, a cursory knowledge of his novel, *Sons and Lovers*.

But with that curious introduction began a marvelous morning of conversation that soon moved on to St. Francis as we sat and talked and sipped sweet vermouth. Lawrence faded rather quickly in this company.

"Oh, father, that poor Pietro Bernardone, to have had such a difficult son. I've scoured libraries for years trying to find one scrap of evidence that Francis and his father, Pietro, were ever reconciled," Nesta lamented.

I determined at that moment that in my book they would be reconciled somehow—and so they are—but only in Francis's fantasy as he imagines the scene in which he and his father are reconciled at a crossroad in his mind:

> And they would be reconciled at some deserted fork in the road, and Pietro would say he understood what Francis had to do that day before the Bishop of Assisi.
>
> Perhaps that was one reason Francis was so often on the road. Perhaps he secretly hoped that his imaginings would come true. And now in the confusion of his dying hours, he could not remember if the

reconciliation really did take place or that rendezvous was kept in his imagination alone.[12]

I'm not sure if Nesta ever read these words. I sent her a copy of the book when the first edition was released in 1972, but I never received a reply. And when I returned to Assisi in 1976 as a staff member of Franciscan Pilgrimage Programs, I went to her apartment to inquire of her and was told by the woman who'd been her companion that the signora had died. I couldn't get any further information from the woman, especially when and where Nesta had died, or maybe my Italian was that inadequate!

Then in 2010 while I was reading Caroline Moorehead's fine biography of Iris Origo, I came across this entry: "Then Nesta de Robeck died and was buried at La Foce...." There was no date, but it was before 1974 when Iris and her husband Antonio celebrated their golden wedding anniversary. So I presumed that Nesta must have died sometime between 1972, when I met her, and 1974, and was buried in the family cemetery at La Foce, the home of the Origos.

Later in doing further research, I found that Nesta de Robeck was born on July 28, 1886, and died in Assisi on February 12, 1983! That would have made her ninety-seven at the time of her death, and she must have gone to La Foce before she died and while Iris, who died in 1988, was still alive. How confused the truth of facts and the truth of memory, even of "the visitable past," can sometimes be. How unreliable our subjective dates.

Nesta's parting words to me when I left Assisi in the summer of 1972 was that she hoped someday I would meet "the extraordinary Iris Origo." I learned later that as a young woman, Nesta, a superb interpreter of Bach, had given music and piano soirees at the Villa Medici in Florence where the young Iris lived with her mother. And later Nesta had taught piano to Gianni, the Origos' only son.

I knew none of this biographical information in 1972, but I did know that there was something extraordinary about this woman, Nesta de Robeck. Her library was richly stocked and helped me immensely. But the most helpful book, which she gave to me as a personal copy, was a copy of her own, *The Life of St. Francis,* a small, almost pamphlet-size paperback, published by the friars at the Edizioni Porziuncola. It was this book that gave me the outline of historical events in the life of St. Francis that were most congenial to the kind of book I was trying to write.

With Nesta's book in hand, I had a chronological template to help me navigate the sometimes confusing chronology of where St. Francis was and when. From that point on, chronology has been the essential prewriting tool for me, as I'm sure it is for any writer trying to negotiate the life of a historical figure. The irony of my own search for Nesta is that the all-important chrono-logical fact of Nesta's own death date was shrouded in mystery until 2013.

How fitting, in one way, that Nesta's death date was for a while, elusive, like the elusive fact that she tried so hard to determine in St. Francis's life, namely, whether or not he was ever reconciled with his father, and what was the date of Francis's birth. Was it 1181 or 1182? Records are lost, records are destroyed, records often elude us. They are not, of course, the whole story, but they provide the template that clarifies and directs the narrative arc that is so important in understanding someone's life. Someday

I'll go to La Foce, to the grave of Nesta de Robeck, and see what date is inscribed there. Someday I'll discover more about St. Francis and St. Clare and what it meant that Clare was the first Franciscan woman.

Chapter Ten

· · ·

THROUGH THE MOIANO GATE

PORTA MOIANO GIVES ONE TIME TO THINK ABOUT ENTERING AND leaving and standing in the middle between the two. There is little traffic there, and the gate itself lies just beyond the edge of the city. It is a more contemplative gate, companionable and consoling for those passages in our lives that are so important that we feel paralyzed between saying good-bye and saying hello.

Because of its distance from the main piazzas of Assisi, there is a feeling of remoteness to Porta Moiano. It's far enough from the action to give you a sense of departing and going to a quiet place to make your exit or entrance unobserved and in the privacy of your thoughts and feelings.

To make a passage through and out of Porta Moiano at night, as Clare did, can be a profoundly contemplative experience. As you leave the city, you automatically turn and look back at the city, which seems to climb layers of houselights up the hill toward the Rocca Maggiore, the fortress that towers over the city and surrounding countryside. So charming is this view that you hesitate and want to return, walk up the streets and steps to the Piazza del Comune for a last evening.

But your time there is now over, and you turn to the gate whose entrance leads into a large space that wants to hold you in its security, its embrace, before you exit onto the dirt road that leads to the paved road that climbs around the city walls toward the lower city of St. Mary of the Angels or toward the uppermost piazza of the city, the Piazza Matteoti.

And still everything about the Porta Moiano seems to want to hold you back, make you stop and reconsider. And you wonder whether there was any hesitation, further consideration, when Clare finally came to this gate, so far from her home beside the Cathedral of San Rufino in the upper part of the city.

The early sources suggest that she was all in a rush to get to Francis and the brothers who lived near the lepers on the plain below. And certainly that must have been the case. But she had to be aware of how momentous this journey away from Assisi— her place, her home—was. Did she go more slowly or ritualize her passage through the gate by stopping inside in order to say good-bye to her city and hello to the vast space of her new life, the exciting but unknown possibilities beyond this gate? Did she perhaps perform a ritual like that of Kristen in Sigrid Undset's great novel of the Middle Ages, *Kristen Lavransdatter*, who when she finally reaches the shrine of St. Olaf at the end of a long pilgrimage, walks three times around the great church before she dares to enter so holy a place?

Clare was about to enter a sacred space made holy by the lepers and the brothers who ministered to them and where she hoped to bring her own ministering heart and hands.

To live outside, beyond, is an experience akin to returning to the original Garden from which man and woman were banished, where they would increase and multiply and live with others of their kind in cities that wall out the wilderness of their banishment. And now Clare was to leave the security of walls and pass into the dark woods of humankind's original banishment whose path would lead her back to the Garden of Eden, the "Paradise" which is refound through letting go of possessiveness and surrendering to God's will in everything, including surrendering to the prohibition to not eat of the fruit of the knowledge which pretends to make us like God.

Only surrender to God will make us like God, surrender like that of Christ's surrender to the Father's will which meant that he was to let go of being possessive about his divinity and then surrender to becoming human out of pure love of his own creatures. That was the journey of Jesus, that was the journey of Clare who was about to make the same journey that Francis and the brothers had made before her. And so she moved purposefully through the Porta Moiano's comforting, womb-like interior to the exit where she passed into the dark and wild woods that are the only way back to Paradise. The way back is the way through.

Chapter Eleven
. . .

THE DORMITORY OF ST. CLARE

ONE DAY, IN THE LATE 1970S, I AND ANOTHER GUIDE WERE leading a group of pilgrims to the church of San Damiano below the Porta Nuova. We were all gathered around the corner spot of the second-floor dormitory where St. Clare died in 1253, twenty-seven years after the death of St. Francis, when suddenly there was a great commotion, and an Italian family came bounding up the steps carrying an obviously very sick young boy. We all instinctively stepped back to make a way to the corner where we'd been praying.

The father came forward quickly, hardly noticing us and gently placed his child on the very spot of St. Clare's passing, made the Sign of the Cross, picked up the child, and hurried down the stairs where the family sped off to the hospital in Perugia, their car horn honking wildly and continuously until we could no longer hear it. We were all still standing dumbstruck. Then spontaneously we began to pray for the healing of the child and for his family.

I had been working on the Franciscan Study Pilgrimage for a few years already when this happened, but it was the first time I had been so dramatically made aware of the healing power of Clare and its being specifically related to this space in the dormitory. I was told that was not a rare occurrence—when someone was rushing toward Perugia to the hospital, he or she would stop and pray in Clare's dormitory before going on. I knew that Francis used to send friars and others to Clare for her healing, and she would make a silent Sign of the Cross over them, and there would be healings that, as I now learned, are still happening today.

Now, programmed into our pilgrimage to San Damiano, there is always a healing service in St. Clare's dormitory that consists of a simple signing with holy oil of each of the pilgrims. Quite a few have experienced some kind of healing, from healing of memories, to healing of animosities and grudges long held, and even of terminal diseases like cancer. I'm sure there have been other healings after the pilgrims returned home that were never reported back to our pilgrimage staff.

St. Clare's dormitory is for this reason one of the most sacred places of Assisi for me. It is where I'm drawn to every year when we return with pilgrims. And when the pilgrims are being led to another part of this holy shrine, I like to sit alone on the windowsill of the dormitory and look down into the center of the courtyard at Clare's well there and lift my eyes up the side of Mount Subasio toward the Carceri, the caves of Francis and the early brothers. I pray easily here. And here I came to know that St. Clare was more than a healer. She was a great Franciscan mystic whose letters open up, as much as letters at that time—with all their formal conventions—could open up the interior life of Clare herself. I can "see" her there writing or dictating a letter.

The monastery of San Damiano lies outside the gates of Assisi on the spur of a hillside that leads down to the ramshackle chapel of La Maddalena where St. Francis worshipped with the lepers.

On the second floor of the monastery of San Damiano above the chapel in a corner of a long open dormitory, Clare di Favarone lies bedridden and is probably dictating a letter to one of her sisters who acts as a scribe. It is 1253, and Clare is fifty-nine years old. She has been ill and often bedridden for twenty-eight years, and yet Clare has carried out all her duties as abbess, as well as tending, when she could, to her own sick sisters.

She has been the faithful keeper of the flame, the personification of Lady Poverty, the mirror of the Poor Christ she and her blessed father Francis embraced and preached in word and in the gestures of their lives from the time God offered them the Gospel of Jesus Christ as their way of life. Francis is gone now; Jesus took him to himself twenty-seven years before, but like Jesus he is alive and well in her heart. They together have held up to their world the mirror of the Christ they'd become, from the moment so long ago now when Clare knelt before Francis and the brothers at the Porziuncola, and Francis cut off her hair and clothed her in the garments of poverty.

She was much younger than Francis and of another class of citizens. Francis was born in 1182 of the rich merchant Pietro Bernardone and his wife, Lady Pica, and Clare was of the noble knightly family of the Offreduccio, born in 1193 of Favarone and Ortolana. How extraordinary that two young people from two disparate classes, a man and a woman, should have come together in a way of living and loving God that would remove all class distinctions, that would embrace even the lepers as their brothers and sisters. How extraordinary that so many men and women would follow in their footsteps from beginnings that were fraught with difficulty and pain, with separation from home and family, with misunderstanding and bitterness from those they loved: Francis from his father Pietro, and Clare from her father Favarone and her uncles of the Offreduccio family.

Her father and uncles would surely have removed her for a while from Assisi had they known that she and her friend Bona had been meeting from time to time with Francis and Brother Philip to discuss her future as a Poor Lady of the Gospel. Their anger knew no bounds when on Palm Sunday night, March 18, 1212, Clare fled her home to join Francis and the brothers at the Porziuncola, becoming thereby the first Franciscan woman.

How Clare would have loved to stay at the Porziuncola when Francis cut off her hair and clothed her in the habit of poverty, but that of course was impossible, and Francis and the brothers led her to the Benedictine monastery of San Paolo delle Abbadesse in nearby Bastia. There, a few days later, what Clare feared would happen, did. Clare's uncle Monaldo and a band of his knights arrived at the monastery to forcibly bring Clare home, but she clung to the altar and they could not remove her, leaving them angry and frustrated.

From San Paolo, Clare went to the church of Sant'Angelo in Panzo on Mount Subasio until Francis and the Bishop of Assisi could arrange for them to move into the small chapel of San Damiano, the church Francis had restored with his own hands and where he prophesied that there would one day be a community of Poor Ladies living within its walls. San Damiano became Clare's home for the rest of her life, and there she and her sisters founded a monastery of the Poor Ladies of San Damiano.

At Sant'Angelo in Panzo there was a group of women living a life of penance together but without professing any officially recognized rule. Here, then, Clare came into contact with a new form of religious life. Also here her younger sister Catherine joined her, and there was another confrontation with the knights of the Offreduccio family. They came in a rage and tried with blows and kicks to forcibly remove her from Sant'Angelo and drag her home. But the sources tell us that Clare began to pray, and Catherine became so heavy they could not budge her, forcing the knights to give up in frustration. Later Catherine received the tonsure of a consecrated virgin from Francis himself, and he gave her a new name, Agnes.

And now it is 1253, many years later, and Clare has been at San Damiano for years. She is writing her fourth letter to another Agnes, Agnes of Prague, the daughter of the King of Bohemia, a princess who could have married the Holy Roman Emperor Frederick II, but instead gave up her claim to royalty for the royalty of Christ. Agnes has renounced wealth and power and followed in the footsteps of Clare by founding a monastery of women in Prague, modeled on the monastery of San Damiano.

Clare began writing Agnes in 1234, reminding her of what she had gained in terms of the royalty Agnes thinks she has given up. And in so writing, Clare revealed her own ecstatic intimacy with the Poor Christ, who is King of the Universe and spouse of Agnes when she contemplates and embraces this poor King.

> Loving Him, You are chaste; touching Him, You are made pure; taking Him to Yourself, You are a virgin. His resources are stronger, His generosity more heavenly, His appearance more beautiful, His love sweeter, and His every grace more attractive.[13]

To write with such power and conviction, Clare has to be writing from her own experience, she who was also a noble woman, the daughter of a knight, who had renounced her noble inheritance to follow in the footsteps of Francis, the son of the rich merchant Pietro Bernardone.

> Therefore, my dearest sister or—as I should say Lady greatly respected, for You are the spouse, mother, and sister of my Lord, Jesus Christ—You are so splendidly distinguished by the banner of inviolable virginity and most holy poverty.[14]

Clare here uses the same image Francis uses from Matthew 12:50, of Agnes now being, through grace, the spouse, mother, and sister of the Lord, Jesus Christ, who has adorned her with undefiled virginity and a most holy poverty. These are Agnes's new raiment.

A year later Clare writes a second letter to Agnes, addressing her, "To the daughter of the King of Kings, to the handmaid of the Lord of Lords, to the most worthy spouse of Jesus Christ, and therefore, a most noble queen, to the Lady Agnes…

> Embrace the poor Christ, O poor virgin. See Him, made contemptible for you and follow, being made contemptible for Him in this world, your Bridegroom, who is the most beautiful of the sons of humanity, for your salvation was made the most vile of men, despised, beaten, and many times whipped all over His whole body, dying on the cross in the depths of anguish, O noble queen, gaze, consider, contemplate, longing to imitate.

> If you suffer with Him, then you will reign with
> Him; grieving with Him, then you will rejoice with
> Him; dying with Him on the cross of torments, then
> you will possess heavenly mansions with Him in the
> splendor of the saints.[15]

Three years later Clare writes again, this time introducing the mirror imagery so important to the troubadours and to other medieval contemplatives like Aelred, who, with the troubadours, believed that the self is mirrored in the Beloved: "The cross of Christ is, as it were, the mirror of the Christian." Clare expands on Aelred's statement, not only seeing herself more clearly in the image of the crucified Christ, but seeing God more clearly as God is mirrored in Jesus Christ.

> So place your mind in the mirror of eternity, place your
> soul in the splendor of glory. Place your heart in the
> figure of the divine substance and, through contempla-
> tion, transform your whole self into an image of the
> Godhead.[16]

Then Clare touches briefly on the pregnancy image she introduced in Letter One.

> Just as the glorious Virgin of virgins materially, so you
> spiritually will certainly be able to carry Him in your
> chaste and virginal body by following in her vestiges
> (especially those of humility and poverty).[17]

Letter Four is the most poetic and ecstatic of the letters, being written in 1253, fifteen years after Letter Three. Clare will die that same year.

Gaze into the mirror everyday, O Queen, Bride of Jesus Christ and constantly see you own face reflected in it.... For in that mirror shine blessed poverty, holy humility, love beyond words....

Turn your mind, I say, to the border of this mirror; to the poverty of Him who was placed in a manger and wrapped in tiny garments. O wonderful humility! O astounding poverty!...

Then, in the center of the mirror, contemplate the holy humility, not to speak of the blessed poverty, the infinite and costly troubles which He took upon Himself to redeem the human race.

At the edges of the same mirror, contemplate the love beyond words through which He chose to suffer on the Tree of the Cross, and, on that same tree, to die the most disgraceful death of any.[18]

The mirror Clare looked into was the San Damiano crucifix. Like her, we look into the mirror of Christ on the cross to see God and to see ourselves—who we are, who we can become. As Christ mirrors us, so we, when we contemplate that mirror, begin to mirror him, who is both God and us when we are transformed by virtue. And it all begins with contemplation.

The cross is both the image of God and of us, only if we let ourselves be transformed by contemplation of the crucified Christ. Clare gazed on the San Damiano crucifix for over forty years, and it transformed her into Christ's mirror.

St. Clare's letters to Agnes of Prague are written with such clarity, conviction, and certainty that one senses she is writing from personal experience. What she says will happen to Agnes when she embraces fully her Divine Spouse, is surely what has happened and is happening to Clare.

As Agnes of Prague could have been the wife of the emperor, but instead embraced Jesus Christ as her spouse, so Clare, too, as the daughter of a knight, could have married into a noble, knightly family, but instead she embraced the poor crucified Christ. Agnes and Clare share similar experiences before they enter the monastery, and Clare is now sharing her own experience in the monastic life at San Damiano. The four letters to Agnes become, in the process, a narrative of the mystical life of St. Clare herself. Were we, for example, to substitute "you" for "I," this is how the first letter would begin:

> I could have enjoyed pomp and honor and high place in this world. It was mine, if I had so wished, with full right to marry in circumstances in accord with my dignity. But I set aside all these things with full intent of heart and unswerving purpose of soul. I have chosen rather most holy poverty and spare support for bodily needs. I have united myself to a Spouse of more noble lineage, the Lord Jesus Christ. He will guard my virginity spotless and untarnished.

Furthermore, as these words make evident, transformation was seen by Clare as a transformation of intimacy whose image is the spousal language of the Song of Songs, as in these words of Clare in her Fourth Letter to Agnes:

> Over and above this, contemplating his
> inexpressible delights, riches and everlasting honours,
> and sighing with the immense longing and love in

your heart, may you cry out: O heavenly
Bridegroom, draw me after you and we will run in the
fragrance of your perfumes!
I will run without stopping
until You lead me into the wine cellar,
until Your left arm be under my head
and Your right will happily embrace me,
You will kiss me
with the happiest kiss of Your mouth.[19]

Clare's language here and elsewhere in the letters is the forceful affective and sensuous language of desire: sighs, crying out, rejoicing, weeping, embracing, tasting, smelling, and kissing. All of which relates directly to the intimate knowledge of Christ effected through contemplation of his image through all the passages of his life. For Clare, to contemplate Christ is to fall in love with him, identify with him, and for love of his love to walk the walk with him, becoming thereby an image, a mirror of the crucified Christ, which is what every Christian mystic is.

In Clare's life the mirror of the crucifix became most real to her in the long illness she endured, bedridden much of the time. Yet, even in suffering she served her sisters, often rising from her bed to minister to their needs, especially those who were ill themselves.

Her penances, too, were so severe that they were a kind of crucifixion. In fact, St. Francis had to admonish her to be more merciful toward her own body. But Clare's penances and sufferings were not, as is sometimes thought of the saints, a form of masochism. They were rather a response of love to a Love that chose to suffer and die that we might know his infinite love for us.

The penances of saints like Clare are also an attempt to join with Christ's redemptive suffering. Clare knew that we all have been reconciled once and for all by Christ, but to enter into that redemptive suffering, and even to lay down one's life for others, makes God's presence among us evident in our own times. Christ died once and for all, but to enter voluntarily into that sacrifice of love with Christ out of our own love of God and neighbor, effects a further outpouring of grace among believers and strengthens the faith of those whose faith is waning. This selfless pouring out of one's life for others for love of Christ can, of course, only be done in God's grace; it is *the* mirror of Christ's continuing presence among us. It was so for Clare; it is so for us today.

Part Three

BEYOND ASSISI

Chapter Twelve

. . .

THE OLIVE TREES OF ASSISI

WHEN ONE LIVES CLOSE TO NATURE AS ST. FRANCIS DID, THERE is, after a while, a rhythm one begins to feel and incorporate into daily life. And though Assisi is a city, its life spills over the walls and confines of the city onto the countryside around. There are fields below and behind the city, and when you exit the train station on a May morning and begin to climb toward Assisi, there are poppies in the fields waving and turned toward the sun rising over Mount Subasio; and in the late summer there are sunflowers, also turned toward Assisi and the rising sun. They seem to be doing homage to the sunlit city. And then there are the olive groves. They, especially, conjure up not only the rhythm of nature that makes its own music, but the very heart of Assisi.

A few years ago when a traffic circle was placed at the approach to the city from the direction of the town of St. Mary of the Angels and from Perugia via the town of Ponte San Giovanni, there was need for a decision about what symbol of Assisi might be placed in the center of this roundabout at the foot of Assisi below the Basilica of St. Francis.

Brilliantly, the city planners chose to transplant an ancient olive tree and place it at the center of the circle. What a perfect icon: something ancient, something organic, a very tree with all the symbolism of the tree in the Judeo-Christian tradition, from the tree of life in the Garden of Eden to the two olive trees in the book of Revelation 11:4: "These are the two olive trees and the two lampstands which stand before the Lord of the earth."

In the mythology of ancient Greece and Rome, the olive tree is associated with peace, as it is also in the Judeo-Christian tradition. Virgil uses the olive branch as a symbol of peace in the *Aeneid*. And the olive branch is first mentioned in Scripture when the dove returns to Noah's ark carrying an olive branch in its beak (see Genesis 8:11). The olive also conjures up anointing and health and antiquity. The *Encyclopedia Judaica* says, "There are trees in Israel estimated to be one thousand years old that still produce fruit. In old age the tree becomes hollow but the trunk continues to grow thicker at times achieving a circumference of twenty feet.... It is an evergreen, and the righteous who take refuge in the protection of God are compared to it."[20] Such olive trees are found on the sides of Mt. Subasio, their hollow trunks twisted, continuing to grow.

Olives themselves provide the oil that is endemic to Italian culture. In Assisi the harvesting and crushing of the olives is one of the most important ongoing seasonal events. It takes place in October and November and reaches back as far as recorded history and beyond, some of the older olive trees covering the hillside that leads to San Damiano. St. Clare and the Poor Ladies of San Damiano would have needed the oil of the olives for cooking, for holy anointing oil, for food. They would have sat in the shade of the trees, felt beneath them the protection of God, the support Clare and Francis both needed in order to found a new order in the Church, a new way of living the Gospel as religious women and men.

What a symbol, then, is the olive tree set at the entrance into Assisi. It is ancient, it is full of biblical resonance, including that of the Garden of Olives where Jesus was betrayed, where he suffered great anguish as he struggled to say yes to his coming passion and death, and where he finally was able to say, "Father, if you are willing, remove this cup from me; yet, not my will, but yours be done" (Luke 22:42).

In the ancient past, in the Middle Ages, in our own time, the olive trees of Assisi continue to grow and to remind us of what they have witnessed and the peace and holy anointing they have come to symbolize.

In a short poem, I have tried to write of the olive trees of San Damiano and their symbolism of support in the lives of Francis and Clare.

THE TREES OF SAN DAMIANO
Clare hears of the death of Francis

The same olive trees still grow
below the city gate on the hill
that slopes to San Damiano.

Old, their gnarled fingers twist
upward to the sun, like my heart
reaching for that sunlit tryst:

you and Philip, me and my friend,
Bona, beneath the silvered leaves that
trembled after the hot sirocco's end.

I look at the gate we saw was closed
to us and what we talked of, beyond
their vision, those who had supposed

us outside what prelates would allow
though we were in the poor God's Body
nailed to the tree that supports me now.[21]

Chapter Thirteen

. . .

PEACE AMID WAR

DURING THE SECOND WORLD WAR, ARMED GUARDS WERE PLACED at all the gates of Assisi twenty-four hours a day. Many years later, I am sitting in the upper garden of Casa Papa Giovanni under the lime trees, watching hang gliders float silently like gossamer down from Mount Subasio onto the fields below Assisi. I am thinking of Don Aldo, remembering him, thanking him.

He was a second father to me, the same age as my biological father, both born in 1914, the beginning of the Great War. He was Don Aldo Brunacci, priest, Canon of the Cathedral of San Rufino. And, with the beloved Bishop Placido Nicolini of Assisi and Colonel Valentin Müller, Commandant of Assisi, he was the savior of no fewer than three hundred Jewish refugees during World War II.

I knew none of this in 1976 when I first met Don Aldo at Casa Papa Giovanni in the bookstore he founded, "Fonte Viva" (Living Water). He was sitting behind the business desk reading a scholarly article that had something to do with the archives of Assisi where Don Aldo worked and did research for years. Franciscan Pilgrimage Programs was just beginning our association with Casa Papa Giovanni where our Franciscan pilgrimages were to be housed for over forty years.

The "Don" of his name is an honorific title for a priest, comparable to "Reverend Father." His baptismal name was Aldo. As a native Assisian he was baptized in the same font, now in the Cathedral of San Rufino, as St. Francis, St. Clare, the early companions of St. Francis, Brother Bernard, Brother Giles, Brother Peter Catanii, Brother Sylvester, and Brother Rufino. The Holy Roman Emperor Frederick II was also baptized in this font, as was St. Gabriel of the Sorrowful Mother.

Don Aldo was a priest deeply inspired by Vatican II. When he turned the former Palazzo Locatelli into a retreat house, he named it *Casa Papa Giovanni*, "The House of Pope John," after Pope John XXIII, who called the Second Vatican Council. His friend Pope Paul VI at one point asked Don Aldo to be the archbishop of Perugia. Don Aldo turned down the offer saying, "I would like to live a few years more!" Which seemed to work. Don Aldo died at the age of ninety-three in his room in Casa Papa Giovanni, showered with honors, including having been made a Righteous Gentile by the State of Israel, offering a prayer in the United States House of Representatives, being memorialized in the Holocaust Museum in Washington, D.C., being awarded the Gaudete Award of St. Bonaventure University, and receiving the highest award of the republic of Italy: Knight of the Great Cross, Order of Merit.

Though I knew Don Aldo from 1976 until his death in 2007 and was aware of much of his distinguished history and of his inestimable contributions to Assisi and to the Jewish refugees there, all that was not what most endeared him to me. It was his friendship and care during several significant moments in my life, including at the death of my father in 1996.

In 1997, I returned to Assisi a few days before the Sunday following the Feast of the Assumption of Mary, which is the day of Assisi's annual commemoration of the dead. Don Aldo was the celebrant at the outdoor Mass in the cemetery of Assisi and asked me to concelebrate with him, an honor and an extremely important moment for me. I realized as we moved through it that this Mass with Don Aldo was bringing closure to the year-long grieving for my father, that my father's remains in the cemetery of Payson, Arizona, were being lifted up with all the remains buried in the cemetery of Assisi. And Don Aldo was there, as he was repeatedly on other occasions over the years.

He was there in 1978 when I began writing my book on St. Clare at Casa Papa Giovanni, and he was there laughing when I got locked out in the rooftop garden one night and spent the whole night staring at the moon and stars and the next morning announced that I'd found the title of the book there: *Clare: A Light in the Garden.*

Later, toward the end of his life, Don Aldo asked me to anoint him with the sacrament of the healing of the sick, and I was able to get there, due to the kindness and generosity of the owner of the bus company we used in Rieti, Italy, where we were leading a group of pilgrims on an Assisi pilgrimage. He drove the three of us pilgrim guides to the hospital in Assisi on a Sunday afternoon and waited until our conversation and the anointing were over.

The endearing thing about Don Aldo is that he never pretended to be anything other than Don Aldo. In time I learned, of course, as one would, who he was to the Assisians and to the Jewish people, the enormous respect accorded him, his place in history as being one of three heroes who ensured that while six million Jews were dying in Europe, not one Jew sheltered in Assisi perished, except one elderly Viennese woman who died of natural causes and whose name Don Aldo changed to Bianca Bianchi so that she could be buried in the Assisi cemetery right under the noses of the Nazis and Fascists there. After the war her son came to Assisi to find her grave, and he and Don Aldo had Mrs. Weiss's real name and the Star of David put onto a new headstone.

Another time, toward the end of the war, the police came to Don Aldo's door just when Professor Emilio Viterbi, a distinguished scientist at the University of Padua, and his wife, Margherita, two Jewish refugees, were in his study. They were seeking a safe place to live. When the police arrived, Don Aldo asked to go and retrieve his breviary in his study where the Viterbis were hiding. He reassured them, told them to stay where they were, then closed the door and was carted off to a makeshift concentration camp in Perugia. The police did not search his house.

Don Aldo was told that his fate would be determined by the fascist prefect Rochi, who was a Nazi collaborator. Fortunately, the Allies were at that time just liberating Rome, and Don Aldo was able to escape from Perugia and find refuge in the Vatican. In a testimonial after the war, Professor Viterbi wrote of his deep gratitude to Don Aldo and the people of Assisi for saving his and his wife's life and the lives of all those who were sheltered there during the war.

One of the main reasons behind the sparing of the Jewish refugees and for the sparing of Assisi itself was that the city of Assisi had been designated a hospital city under the command of a devout Catholic and medical doctor from Eichstätt, Germany, Colonel Valentin Müller. And this is how that came about.

On September 9, 1943, when the Germans occupied Assisi, there was the great fear and real possibility that Assisi would be caught in the crossfire between the Germans and the advancing Allied Forces, but almost immediately several buildings were commandeered as hospitals. Then, through the efforts of the Custos of the Basilica of St. Francis, Fr. Bonaventura Mansi; the Bishop of Assisi, Giuseppe Placido Nicolini; the Mayor of Assisi, Arnaldo Fortini; and the sympathetic director of the German military hospitals in Assisi, Colonel Valentin Müller, the whole city was declared a hospital city, a designation that, at least on paper, made Assisi out of bounds for German and Allied bombing and military engagements. And in the end the city and its precious shrines were never harmed. It remained, as St. Francis's blessing wanted it to be, a city of peace.

But it was Colonel Valentin Müller, who at the end, was the real savior of the city. He was greatly concerned, as the war in Italy drew to an end, that the retreating German troops might occupy the city, although the German Commander in Italy, Field Marshall Albert Kesserling, had assured him that he had issued an order forbidding military troops from entering Assisi. But Müller was still concerned, and he placed guards around the clock at all the gates of the city to prevent troops from entering the city.

Then, in the second week of June, 1944, as the Allied troops drew nearer, Müller received orders to evacuate the two thousand German wounded, as well as the hospital personnel, from Assisi. Müller took personal charge of the evacuation in order to ensure that no buildings, furnishing, equipment, and so forth, were harmed in the evacuation.

When the approaching Allies were on the outskirts of the nearby city of Foligno, the German rear guard was at St. Mary of the Angels below Assisi. Fearing that they might retreat to Assisi, Müller again reinforced the gates and on June 15 positioned himself outside the main gate of the city. He could hear the sounds of demolition in the valley and could see buildings being set on fire by angry SS troops.

The next day some of the SS troops came to Assisi, and Müller and the SS engaged in a heated debate that fortunately lasted long enough for Müller to convince the German rear guard to abandon the city. The city was saved! And on June 16, Colonel Müller and his division set out on the road leading north from Assisi.

In 1982, the eighth centenary of the birth of St. Francis, a delegation from Assisi, led by Don Aldo, went to Eichstätt, Germany, to place olive branches from the hillsides of Assisi on Colonel Müller's grave on whose tombstone is carved the façade of the Basilica of St. Francis.[22]

The olive trees of Assisi figure in this gesture of homage to a man of peace who helped save the city of Assisi. And how fitting that this ancient hill town that has been a place of healing for so many was itself saved because it was a center of healing and safe refuge during World War II. And that dimension of healing continues in the Assisi of today where so many, including myself, have come over the years, hoping and praying for healing.

The little chapel of San Damiano that St. Francis rebuilt with his own hands and where Clare founded a Franciscan Order of contemplative women and where she lived most of her life, was named after the early Roman martyrs, Sts. Cosmas and Damian, twin brothers and physicians. Clare continued the tradition of healing at this spot along the Flaminian Road, which even in Roman times was a wayside shrine. She healed many of those sent to her by St. Francis, she brought healing to me as I prayed in her dormitory and learned there that we are healed not just by a place like Assisi but by the people there, as well, by people like Don Aldo Brunacci, whose friendship was a healing balm for me for almost forty years.

Assisi, its shrines and its people. Assisi, a place of healing that brings joy. Assisi, a place of wonder. Assisi, a people who welcome those who pass through the gates of their city. Assisi, home of Don Aldo, whom I still see in my mind's eye:

> Echoes pulsate from the stones
> where I last saw Don Aldo,
>
> a frail 92, his cane
> gently tapping away from me
>
> toward the Piazza del Comune
> at the end of Via San Paolo.
>
> I watched him walking, it seemed,
> forever, and the piazza—like
>
> the Jewish refugees he sheltered
> and saved from harm—kept
>
> receding from his determined will.
> I see him walking still,
>
> his short shuffle out of step
> among friends and passersby.[23]

Chapter Fourteen

...

OF CAVES

IT WAS, I REMEMBER, A SPRING DAY, THE ILEX AND HOLM OAK along the way opening their green welcome to my slow progress up the mountainside. I had left by the Porta dei Cappuccini, the Capuchin Gate, as one usually does to walk to the Carceri, the small caves that the young Francis entered and prayed in when he was in earnest to discern what God was asking of him.

He used to take a friend with him, saying only that he had found a great treasure. He would leave his companion outside when he entered the cave to see if the treasure was still there.

And here I was, making the same journey up the mountain with no companion beside me but the spiritual presence of Francis and my imagination. What was that treasure, I wondered, and would it still be there for me? I was in my thirty-ninth year and making my first pilgrimage as a pilgrim guide for Franciscan Pilgrimage Programs. I had been to the Carceri before, had lived with the friars there for three days, when I was writing *Francis: The Journey and the Dream*, but that journey up the mountain was by car, switch-backing rapidly up the winding, paved road to the gates of the hermitage. There wasn't much reflection on that speedy journey whose goal was to "get there."

Now, however, I was walking and looking and thinking, noticing with each step that I was leaving the world of Assisi whose values and preoccupations were much the same as those the young Francis left behind to find the treasure in a dark cave on a mountainside.

He, too, had to pass through a gate above the city, but was it this very gate I had taken? There was another medieval gate nearby, the Porta Perlici at the foot of the Rocca Maggiore, the site of the castle fortification, the original version of which had been torn down by the citizens a few years before when they rose up against imperial power to assert their own rights and form a commune run by representatives chosen by the people themselves.

In any case, the treasure was found away from all the struggles and wars and business competition of Assisi, away from family feuds, from jockeying for power and influence and wealth, away from the divisions between nobles and ordinary people, between upper and lower classes, between the more privileged upper geography of the city and the less privileged and often disenfranchised lower part of the city, away from the struggle and frequent armed conflict between pope and emperor, bishop and mayor, abbots and diocesan authorities.

By walking out of one of the upper gates of the city toward Mount Subasio's caves, Francis was symbolically rehearsing his final departure from the Porta San Giacomo to walk in the footsteps of Jesus. He had found this Jesus in a cave above the city and would follow him toward those who lived below the city. Always, though, his whole life long, he would walk up whatever mountain he was near in order to pray in its caves until he found again the Jesus who would then accompany him down the mountain of prayer to where the poor lived on the plain below a walled city that closed its gates to the marginal, the outcast, the poor, and the contagiously ill.

As I walked, reflecting and carefully trudging over stones, I tried to keep to the path and away from the poisonous snakes, the vipers that dwell in the woods one has to pass through on the way to the mouth of the cave where lies the treasure Jesus left on the mountain when he went aside to pray.

As the sun rose higher over Mount Subasio, I could feel the sweat beginning to drip from my body, even though it was early morning and the air was not yet muggy or brilliant in the scorching sun's rays. The effort of the climb, though making me sweat, was at the same time taking on an almost mantra-like rhythm to the upward placing of one foot in front of the other as I looked down most of the time to be sure of my footing. I could have stayed on the paved road, but there was no mystery in that, no identification with the young Francis who would have known the shortcuts through the woods on paths others had forged before him; for the caves of Mount Subasio had been made holy as the prayer sites of hermits and others for centuries before the time of Francis.

When I would pause in a clearing to view the panorama below, Assisi seemed but a pile of rocks interrupting the eyes' sweep toward the breathtaking Valley of Spoleto spread out below. I wondered why Francis did not pray *on* the mountaintop contemplating this awesome panoply below, but instead prayed *in* the mountain, inside, within? It was, I concluded, because that was where the treasure was buried, beneath the surface of the mountain. And as beautiful as all of nature was, it couldn't really be seen, except with eyes in-Spirited by the journey into the dark cave whose lack of an external light source, somehow facilitated another light that, like the light of a medieval miniature illumination, began to glow from within.

Is that what I would find when I finally reached the caves of St. Francis and later on, the caves of the other Lesser Brothers who followed Francis to the mountain in order to enter their own dark caves of discovery and illumination?

Something did happen to me that day—no big or small epiphany in one of the caves—but instead the realization of how difficult is the climb to where the treasure lies. It was a realization, too, of the necessity of climbing an inner mountain and then descending to the cave within it. This was confirmed for me later in other caves of St. Francis.

There were, for example, the caves of La Verna where Francis prayed in preparation for the surprise and incredible gift of the sacred stigmata; there was the cave at Greccio above the Rieti Valley where Francis began to popularize the live Christmas crèche; of Fonte Colombo above the same valley, the cave where Francis wrote his final Rule for the Brothers; there also was the cave of Poggio Bustone, where Francis was visited by the angel who assured him that all his sins were forgiven; and there were the caves of many Franciscan hermitage sites of Umbria and Tuscany and beyond. And always, it seemed, there was the same dynamic: up and into a mountain to find the treasure that enables the descent to the roads and plains below where Francis and the early brothers would preach to and work among those left by the wayside by others' headlong journey toward possessions and power and security. One passed through the gates of whatever had walled one in toward the real gate: the entrance to the cave within.

And all these gates led me finally to return to the entrance of another "cave" where St. Francis is buried, in a crypt inside a hill outside the original walls of Assisi. It is a cave that, like all the others, reveals to us the treasure which is the Gospel of Jesus Christ that sends us forth from Assisi, as it did Francis, to return to our original true place and find there the way into our own mountain where we find the Spirit of God who will send us forth, beyond our own protective walls, to find the poor among us and beyond us, beyond, at least, our former seeing and living.

And at some point we have to return to Assisi, at least in memory or imagination, and pass through the Capuchin Gate, hopefully in a springtime of the soul, and begin the slow ascent of Mount Subasio and reenter the caves of St. Francis looking for renewed energy and inspiration, for the silence and solitude that send us back to the plain below, to those, especially, who have no lightsome place to lay their head.

Chapter Fifteen

. . .

PORTA DEI CAPPUCCINI:
THE CAPUCHIN GATE

I'M SITTING AT MY WINDOW IN ROOM 10 OF CASA PAPA GIOVANNI on the Via San Paolo. It's on the second floor, which in Europe generally means three floors up from the ground floor. It's airy here looking out over the tiled roofs to the hills on the other side of the Valley of Spoleto. Pigeons strut the roof tiles directly opposite mine, and images of over forty years drift through my memory.

They slide across my mind like photos that one slides across the screen of a smart phone. I surf them, waiting for an image that arrests my attention; toward the middle of the slides in my mind, a rooftop stops my surfing. It is of the roof tiles of the chapel and cave where St. Francis prayed in what is now the hermitage of the Carceri on the side of Mount Subasio. It juts out from the mountain, clinging precariously, it seems, lest it fall into the deep ravine below. Nearby, next to a stone bridge, is one of the trees where St. Francis supposedly spoke to the birds perched in its branches, inviting them to praise the Creator, the Most High, all-powerful, good Lord.

When you finally reach the hermitage of the Carceri, after a long, steep walk from the Porta dei Cappuccini, you pass through an open iron gate onto a dirt road that leads up a gently rising slope to the hermitage itself with its small courtyard and well. Off of this courtyard are three entrances, one to the modern chapel, one to the fifteenth-century chapel, and one to the fifteenth-century refectory and friars' cells built by St. Bernardine of Siena. When you enter the small fifteenth-century chapel, you see that it serves as an ante-chapel, a sort of vestibule, to prepare you to enter the smaller, thirteenth-century Mary chapel where Brother Leo said Mass for Francis and the early brothers who lived in the caves a short distance away.

To the right of this small chapel is a steep stone staircase that leads to the cave where Francis prayed and slept, which in turn leads through another stone passageway that is tight and, for some, semi-claustrophobic, to a narrow threshold door that leads outside to a small courtyard.

Without realizing it at first, you sense that you have made a profound and moving passage, through several thresholds, that makes you feel like you've traveled with and into the soul of St. Francis. You have ritualized his mountain experience here at the Carceri—the "prisons"—so named, you know now, because these small caves that wind through subterranean tunnels, one into another, are like small stone prisons that only a passage *through* will bring you back into the light where the sun glints off the tiles of the hermitage itself and where a sharply deep ravine threatens your passage up a further stone bridge that leads to the path above.

There were no tiled roofs over the hermitage, the cave, of Francis when he lived and prayed here. The whole complex was built afterward, beginning in the fifteenth century with St. Bernardine of Siena, in order to enshrine and provide a way for others to enter and pass through the thresholds of St. Francis's outer and inner journeys: mountain caves to ways through and out of the "prisons" of the earth that mirror those inner prisons of our own making, the prisons of our unenlightened hearts.

How beautifully the present hermitage of the Carceri does just that for one who enters and walks its passageways prayerfully, attending to and being present before its stone mysteries.

A sudden fast-forward disturbs my reverie, and I look up. Twilight and a swoosh of swallows erase the tiled roofs. My eyes try to follow them, but they're too fast, too erratic, seemingly bent on evading my eyes' camera, my mind's need to arrest their to and fro food-seeking and wing-stretching flight after day's long, contemplative roost.

*　*　*

I saw it first on my walking climb to the Carceri. Passing through the metal gate of the present-day hermitage, stopping and looking up, was the first time I really "saw" Mount Subasio— not just as the place where Francis and the brothers prayed, but as a mountain, something to aspire to in its own right. I wanted to climb it, go to the summit, and find there the ecstasy of being between earth and heaven.

So preoccupied had I been with Assisi that I couldn't see beyond it to the goal of everything, that other threshold, that border where earth and heaven meet. The mountain is the symbol of that apogee in the soul where we meet God. This is not to denigrate or dismiss what is below, but to lift it up and give thanks to God for all that God has made; to bless it and praise God and see that everything is good because it comes from God and ultimately leads us beyond itself to the God who made it and redeems it. What is below makes the mountain. It does not rest on air, on spirit, but on matter, which is the mountain's way to the heights of union with God. The mountain affirms incarnation, the entering of God into all that God has made.

And so, even though my immediate goal was the caves of Francis and his brothers, I knew that soon I must go all the way to the top of Mount Subasio. In the end I walked one day only to the Carceri, then hitched a ride to the stunning summit of the mountain—thereby, sadly missing the way of matter—to its apogee. But even the car ride seemed a long detour from the Carceri. I had become preoccupied with caves.

Chapter Sixteen

. . .

CROSSINGS

When I am walking I fall deep into dreams,
I float through fantasies and find myself inside
unbelievable stories. I literally walk through
whole novels and films and football matches.[24]

—Werner Herzog

WE WALK MOST OF OUR LIVES, AND WE'RE ALMOST DAILY CROSSING thresholds of one kind or another that we take for granted or simply don't notice, except perhaps as a marker on the way to wherever we're going to or coming from. And that is the natural, ordinary way it is with us. But sometimes, as on a pilgrimage, we are more aware, more attentive to the environment and geography of the journey.

Even on journeys at sea we can, if we are attentive, sense when we are crossing something: a midpoint of longitude, a place where something significant or momentous has happened, like the sinking of the *Titanic*. The whole ocean surface itself is a threshold between its depths and the element of air. We sail on a border between air and water, the ocean itself being a wet border between air and the earth below the sea over whose pitch black surface strange eyeless creatures glide.

We live with all kinds of borders, between inner and outer; the material and the spiritual; the past, present, and future. Borders happen in us and to us, and the art of living is the art of attentiveness to what is, what happens without us, what happens in and to us.

We couldn't bear, of course, to be simultaneously aware of everything. One thing alone is sufficient, for everything is contained in every single thing. God showed the medieval mystic, Julian of Norwich, for example, a little thing, the size of a hazelnut on the palm of her hand and said that everything is contained in it. And she understood that this little thing contained three truths: that God made it, that God loves it, and that God sustains its existence.

And so we begin by learning to look at one thing only until, as the Jesuit poet Gerard Manley Hopkins says, it looks back at us. In that simple interchange we learn to see other things. We develop the habit of looking closely, deeply at and into things.

Such looking presumes a calm and peace, which may precede the looking but most often is found in the very act of looking. Close looking at the things of God's creation brings peace unless what we are looking at is chaotic, violent, broken, damaged. Then peace comes only when we've done something, however small, to heal, to reorder, to "make beautiful," as St. Bonaventure says, "that which has been deformed."

In the case of a human being, even a smile of acceptance and love can begin to heal and beautify what seemed irreparably harmed or distorted. Beauty, after all, does remain in the soul of the damaged person; it can still shine forth in the body. There are all kinds of beauty, and love reveals them when it gazes reverently on any created thing.

St. Francis was a man who seemed to erase borders, who walked back and forth between Assisi and the world outside its walls, thereby healing and reconciling different worlds and values, the outer and the inner. Unlike the enclosed spaces of cloistered monks, the cloister of the brothers was the world itself.

And St. Francis did spend almost half of his life on and in the mountain, and the other half he spent on the road entering and leaving cities. He founded some twenty-two hermitages on mountains. As Jesus walked up the mountain to pray, then descended and moved among the people, so did Francis and the early brothers, discovering, contemplating, and sanctifying new places, as they continued to walk beyond their own history, as do we if we learn to walk into and out of our own Assisi as pilgrims.

To be a pilgrim means to let go of the need to be attached to one place only. Space, in turn, then becomes the place that home usually is. It requires traveling lightly, open to and expecting surprises and blessings from those we meet along the way—a foretaste of journey's end.

I've come to this description from almost forty years of walking the pilgrim's way to Assisi and in and out of its streets, and up the hill beyond to Mount Subasio. Not always actually walking, but also getting to Assisi by air and land and sea, by railroads and paved roads and dirt paths—but always trying to walk part of the way and to maintain the rhythm of contemplative walking all along the way.

I've walked through the gates of Assisi again and again, for it is only by walking through the gate that we really experience the gate: its threshold, midpoint, and exit. It is only by walking that we can remain inside as long as it takes to know viscerally, as well as intellectually, what the experience of passage through is.

At each stage of our lives walking has its own difficulty and is a different kind of passage. When we're young, we are only learning to walk. By the time we reach middle age, even though we've become experts at walking, it can be hard to slow our steps long enough to be aware and be present to what we're doing. In old age, we cannot walk as we did when we were younger, and we know in our whole being what it means to surrender, to accept limitations and physical difficulties. We continue to walk and pass through the gates of growing older on the pilgrim way.

The gate where I've most experienced the stages of my life in Assisi is Porta Nuova, the New Gate, because it is the main entrance to the city center and because it is the way down to and up the steep ascent from San Damiano, outside the walls, to the Piazza Comune, in the middle of the city; and it is that walk to and from San Damiano that most seems to bless my way.

When I was younger, I could actually sprint up the hill from San Damiano to the Porta Nuova; and the passage through the gate seemed winged. Now I stroll up the hill, pause for a rest before entering the gate, and wait for a break in the traffic so that I can pause again inside the gate before strolling to the Piazza of Saint Clare, hands folded behind my back like an Italian grandfather on his evening walk that the Italians call a *passegiata* around the fountain in the Piazza of St. Clare.

So now Porta Nuova feels anything but new. It is the old gate of my first experience of Assisi when I passed through it in the small bus that took me from the train station on the plain below to the Piazza of St. Clare where I then hoisted on my backpack and walked briskly up the steep steps to St. Anthony's Guest House.

That was my first pilgrimage, and I was alone and thirty-five years old on a dark night in March, 1972.

And what was then new for me is now older, but the passages are the same. And when I make the most important passages, I try to walk, for with Werner Herzog, "when I am walking I fall deep into dreams, I float through fantasies and find myself inside unbelievable stories...."

Chapter Seventeen

...

ORDINARY GATES

I AM SITTING IN BAR SENSI HAVING A MORNING CAPPUCCINO AND a brioche and looking out past the pastries, all homemade by the owner, to the street outside where cars are unloading school children. Mothers are leading little uniformed munchkins by the hand through the small arch that leads to the street below, which runs through a small piazza near the *staletta*, or stable, where St. Francis is believed to have been born, to the school down the steps from the piazza.

This is the neighborhood of the boy Francis whose family home is now superimposed by the Chiesa Nuova, the "New Church," built largely with funds provided by Philip III of Spain. The first stone was laid on September 17, the Feast of the Stigmata of St. Francis, 1616, the same year that Miguel de Cervantes and William Shakespeare died. Its architecture is that of the Greek cross with a central dome and four small ones surrounding it. The area of the sanctuary is supposedly the area of the family bedrooms. In a niche under one of the small pillars is a small faux "prison" structure where Francis's father, Pietro Bernardone, is supposed to have locked up his son when Pietro returned from a cloth-buying journey and found Francis walking about the city like a mad man begging stones to restore the small chapel of San Damiano outside the walls.

All this domesticity—that is what surrounds this area that you enter from the Piazza del Comune just up the street from the "Ordinary Gate," the Gate of San Giorgio, which is today a simple arch connecting two sides of the street.

School, growing up, a father and his son, a mother and her son, joy and misunderstanding and conflict; pride and disappointment in one's offspring; growing away from one's parents, growing out of the strictures of one's home town: the stuff of our ordinary lives.

The boy Francis would have gone out into the street where today the bakery trucks and the cars with children unload their precious cargoes. He would have turned right to walk toward the Porta San Giorgio, which led to the church and school of San Giorgio which today is replaced by the gothic Basilica of St. Clare. Nothing remains of the original church except a wall one can see in the present chapel where the original San Damiano cross hangs. The cross was brought here to St. Clare's Basilica by the Poor Clares when they moved inside the walls of Assisi to live in the monastery attached to the Basilica of St. Clare.

You kneel before the San Damiano cross, and there ahead and beyond the cross is a wall of frescoes, one of which depicts St. Clare. This ancient, frescoed wall of the church of San Giorgio is within the cloister and, like so much of the medieval world, is just beyond our reach.

I call the Gate of San Giorgio the Ordinary Gate because it was through this gate, coming and going, that Francis lived his ordinary life as a boy. Here he played with his friends, here he learned his letters, which amounted to what we would call today elementary education.

Also, it is through this Ordinary Gate that one passes to enter the Piazza del Comune, the Piazza of the Commune, of the ordinary people who wait for the bakery trucks, who drop children off and pick them up from school.

When I come here to Bar Sensi, I feel close to the city's heartbeat, to the locals who patronize this same bar, who eat the pancaciato, the nut roll that makes a midmorning cappuccino a treat to look forward to. It is a place that becomes the "coffee bar next door" when you are away from home. There is a familiarity here, a coziness that is comfortable and comforting and is reached through one of those ordinary gates we take for granted or don't even notice we are passing through.

Part Four

LONGING

Chapter Eighteen
. . .

PORTA PERLICI:
GATE OF THE WOUNDED WARRIOR

THIS IS THE GATE THAT MAKES ME THINK OF WAR AND ITS
futility: Porta Perlici, the Perlici Gate. Ironically, prior to 1240
this gate, just off the Piazza Matteoti, the uppermost piazza of
Assisi, was a hospice for pilgrims and the sick. But in 1240 the
Canons of the Cathedral moved the hospice to the Church of
San Giorgio, the present-day site of St. Clare's Basilica.

An inscription on the Porta Perlici indicates that the original gate was built in 1199 to provide access to the Marches of
Ancona. It is the last gate through which Francis reentered Assisi
when he became ill on the road. And every year on the Saturday
before the first Sunday of September, a group of "knights" from
Assisi go to Satriano. Returning the following day in a make-
believe cortege, the *Cavalcata*, they celebrate the return of
Francis.

Porta Perlici is the nearest gate to the Rocca Maggiore, one of
the major centers of power at the time of St. Francis. It was occupied from 1174 to 1198 by a German count, who represented
the Holy Roman Emperor who was intent on preserving the
power of Assisi's feudal knights, of whom Clare's father was one.

There were three other centers of power in Assisi, beginning
with the earliest, the first Cathedral, Casa di Santa Maria (House
of Holy Mary), which from the Middle Ages onward became St.

Mary Major. Now, as in the Middle Ages, it is adjacent to the residence of the Bishop of Assisi, who was the foremost ecclesiastical feudal Lord at the time of St. Francis. Another center of power was the area around the new Cathedral of San Rufino and the area on the western spur of Mount Subasio near the Porta San Giacomo a Muro Rupto (St. James of the Breached Wall). In this area were the families of the priors and canons of the new cathedral who were bent on curbing the power of the Bishop of Assisi. And finally, there was the Piazza del Comune which, as indicated in an earlier chapter, was the area in the middle of town that housed the merchants of the rising middle class.

So, when Francis returns, a wounded warrior from his forays into the world beyond Assisi as the "Herald of the Great King," it is fitting and symbolic that he passes through the Porta Perlici, which had begun as a hospice for the sick! He proceeds down the hill past the Cathedral of San Rufino, across the Piazza del Comune and the site of his boyhood home, to the old Cathedral of St. Mary Major where he rests in the bishop's palace. In that way he crosses all the centers of power, blessing them, then leaving them behind a short time afterward as he is carried on a litter out the Porta Moiano and down the hill, stopping along the way to bless his city in the distance before proceeding to the Porziuncola where, on October 3, 1226, lying on the bare ground, Francis passes into paradise.

Assisi is a good place to think about war; there was so much of it here. War was here before St. Francis, during his lifetime, and years after he passed into eternity. And this gate is a good place to focus on Francis and his forays into war and back again to learn to live as a man of peace.

There is a striking, larger than life, bronze statue situated at the outer perimeter of the piazza of the Upper Basilica of St. Francis. It depicts the young Francis bent over his horse in seeming defeat as he returns from Spoleto where he'd gone in search of knightly glory.

He'd gone to war before with horse and lance in the war between Assisi and Perugia, in which he was taken prisoner for a year. He came home a broken man and spent much of that year recuperating physically and mentally, all the while preparing himself for what he thought he had to do: get back on his horse and try again.

Then one night he dreamed he was in a large castle hall on whose walls hung many shields. And when he asked whose shields they were, he heard a voice:

"They are for you and your followers."

And when Francis awakened, he presumed that it was time for him to return to war, a reborn knight.

And so, when he heard of an opportunity to join the papal forces in Apulia under the command of the Frenchman, Walter of Brienne, to fight against the Holy Roman Emperor, Francis again set forth with other of Assisi's young men to travel to southern Italy. But something happened the very first night out while they were camped at Spoleto, a day's journey from Assisi. He again fell ill, and again he heard a voice:

"Francis, who is it better to serve, the Master or the servant?"

"The Master," Francis answered.

"Then why are you going forth to serve the servant instead of the Master?"

"Lord, what do you want me to do?

"Return home to Assisi, and there you will learn what you are to do. The vision you had in your dream of shields you must understand in a new way."

And so it was that Francis's fellow soldiers went on their way to Apulia, and Francis returned home, a seeming coward, again a sick man, and withal totally clueless about what he was to do.

He roamed the hillsides, he visited ramshackle chapels outside the city walls, and he had two experiences that showed him what kind of knight he was to be. One day when he was riding his horse below the city walls, he met a leper and was moved to dismount his horse, go up to the leper, and not only give him coins, but to embrace the leper.

And when he did, he felt not revulsion but sweetness of soul and body. And when he mounted his horse again and turned to wave to the leper standing on the side of the road, there was no one there. And it was revealed to Francis that he had embraced Jesus Christ.

This was to be the new chivalry: to protect and embrace the most abject of people, the poorest of the poor. In that he would be a true knight whose battles were within him. He was to fight valiantly to overcome shame and fear and to work among others who had been rejected by their society. His triumphs would not be his but the Lord's whom he served: Jesus Christ, the Master who had spoken to him in his dream at Spoleto.

The second defining moment came one day when he was praying before the cross in the rundown chapel of San Damiano outside the walls. And as he prayed before the cross for enlightenment about what else he must do to fulfill the will of his Master, he heard a voice from the crucifix suddenly speak to him:

"Francis, go and repair my house which, as you see, is falling into ruin."

And Francis, thinking the message to be literal, began to repair San Damiano with his own hands. In that way, beginning with begging stones, Francis started to also restore the Church itself; for in rebuilding actual churches (he rebuilt three), he was at the same time rebuilding what was falling into ruin spiritually. The two go together: working physically with one's hands in solidarity with others and embracing those who have been excluded, bringing them, too, into the circle of work and love.

This is the "Wounded Warrior" who at the beginning returned bent over his horse's neck in seeming defeat. This is the knight of Christ who, as he lay dying, was carried through the Porta Perlici into the Assisi he had left as a young man to rebuild the Church by serving its Master. This is the returning warrior who crossed through all the gates and places of power in Assisi to bless them and wish them peace. This is the would-be knight who, in leaving war, entered the peace that surpasses all understanding.

Chapter Nineteen

. . .

WHEN THE GATES DON'T SPEAK

SOMETIMES WHEN WE ARE ON PILGRIMAGE AND COME TO THE place of our journeying, we are let down or feel more empty than full. We wonder what is missing. What have we done wrong? What haven't we understood when we made our way to a powerful place of pilgrimage like Assisi?

We probably have done nothing wrong, of course, and what we're feeling may have causes other than the pilgrimage we're making. Or it could be that the feeling of emptiness is what God wants us to experience in order to understand what the peace and joy of Assisi really is. Maybe God is allowing us to experience emptiness in order that God can fill it with God's own fullness.

It involves not being scandalized, as moderns often are, by the extreme asceticism, the severe deprivations and penances of St. Francis. Some even see a kind of masochism or self-hatred in the way of the cross that he embraced, and they try to find peace in Assisi without looking at this dimension of the man who left this city to follow the poor crucified Christ.

The very term "way of the cross" is the answer to why St. Francis did what he did. He did not choose suffering for suffering's sake; he *embraced* the cross as the sign and fulfillment of the self-emptying Christ. St. Francis had nothing when he walked out of Assisi, having renounced his father and the values of his city. He didn't know exactly where he was going or what he was to do. But he knew that God would show him what he was to do.

What he did see, though, was that the emptying gesture of the Incarnation of God is *the* way of making a sacred space for God in oneself. And rather than emphasizing the emptying, he emphasized the embracing. He embraced the *poor* Christ; he embraced the lepers. As he says in his *Testament*, "When I was in sins, the sight of lepers nauseated me beyond measure; but then God himself led me into their company, and I worked mercy with them. And once I became acquainted with them, what had previously nauseated me became a source of spiritual and physical consolation for me."[25]

The poverty of St. Francis, then, is in the "penance" of overcoming fear and revulsion to *embrace* what is without love or affirmation. And then the fullness returns. We make an empty space for God when we embrace those who are rejected because of our own selfishness. And that empty space is filled with God. If we feel empty, there may be someone we need to reach out to, be reconciled with, and embrace, someone we've rejected or feel repulsed by. Even the intent to do so can lift one's spirits and give one a goal, the goal of conversion, of turning our lives around and letting God embrace us so that we can embrace others in turn. And this, too, happens to those who come to Assisi. They feel they have to return and do something that will make a difference for good in the lives of others.

Every penance Francis undertook was really a part of building God's kingdom. His penances were in order to make a space within for the sweet "emptiness" of Christ to enter—an "emptiness" that is really a fullness, the fullness of God himself who entered our humanity by emptying himself of divinity so that he could become fully one of us. We then enter into divinity by emptying ourselves of every illusion that tells us that fulfillment is being filled with something other than God, with a sweet feeling, for example, when we pass through the gates of Assisi. It is not about a sweet feeling but about a change of heart and life.

When St. Paul tells us that Christ emptied himself of divinity, he is saying that Christ emptied himself of clinging to divinity: "who, though he was God, did not think of equality with God as something to *cling* to" (Philippians 2:6, *NLT,* emphasis added). So it is with us: It is of possessiveness that we need to be emptied and not of our humanity; we need to be emptied even of the possessiveness that *clings* to spiritual consolation or ecstatic feelings of the presence of God.

St. Francis was so in love with God as revealed in Jesus Christ, that he strove with the courage and gallantry of the true knight he had previously wanted to be, in order to make his whole life the quest of that emptying of possessiveness that invites the embrace of Christ, who in embracing our poverty is filled with sweetness. In the same way, Francis embraced the poverty of the leper and was filled with the sweetness of God.

To enter the gates of Assisi and remain there a while, and then to exit again is to know that you are being sent by what Francis did here and didn't do here. It is to know that you are about more than yourself and that your true self waits for you to reach out and live the Gospel among those who are most in need.

Chapter Twenty
. . .

SILENCE AND SOLITUDE

"THERE WAS," SAID CLAUDIO ABBADO, "A CERTAIN SOUND TO snow. It did not come from walking on it. If you stood on a balcony, too, you could hear it. A falling sound, fading away to nothing, *pianissimo,* like a breath. You could hear it only if you listened to what some supposed was silence."[26]

Silence. Solitude. How large they are, how enlarging. This I learned in Assisi the first time I lived there. Those three months kept expanding, opening up because every day I could sit at my desk, knowing I would not be disturbed. And it would be that way day after day for three months.

Every day as I sat writing after breakfast, the world of St. Francis would open up like a page from a magical book whose words became scenes and dialogues in a 3-D movie that took place centuries before.

Silence.... Solitude.... They fill in the sentences between the periods on the page. I remember little of what came to me during those solitary times. Perhaps what came to me is now in the pages of the book I was writing then.

I do not remember how the writing came. It just seemed to flow from my pen, from the silent contemplation of things I would see as I walked the streets of Assisi. None of the Assisians knew me then, so I could sit and watch people or walk and see without anyone really seeing me. Then suddenly a scene or an overheard conversation or a face would become medieval, and I would know what I would write the next morning.

In the evening I would walk down the Via Galeazzo Alessi to the piazza to listen to the fountain that was there when Francis lived near the Piazza del Comune. Then, sitting on the fountain steps, I would face the well-lit piazza bars, and sometimes there would be silence, and I would be alone in the darkness of the Middle Ages when all the people were asleep, having gone to bed when darkness fell.

Someone once said that the streets of Assisi awaken the imagination. And so it was for me day in and day out during that incredibly gifted time when I was young and in love with the very air of the city.

Perhaps it was anonymity that facilitated all this. For when I was observing and walking through the streets imagining, I never wore my Franciscan habit. That would have immediately made me someone to be seen, someone to talk to and ask directions of, someone who could perhaps speak English and tell them about St. Francis and the city and the times in which he lived. All of which would have broken the silent spell, ruined the writing by talking.

Some may not understand the writer's near obsession with the need for solitude and silence, but it is essential. Ernest Hemingway wrote in his Nobel acceptance speech, "The writer must write what he has to say, not speak it." And in fact, Hemingway did not actually deliver his two-minute speech. He asked the American ambassador to Sweden to read it for him because he was seriously ill, recovering from two back-to-back plane crashes that almost took his life. He did, however, record it at a later time—the solitary writer speaking into the solitary microphone.

As Hemingway put it in his speech, "Writing, at its best, is a lonely life. Organizations for writers palliate the loneliness, but I doubt if they improve his writing.... For he does his work alone and if he is a good enough writer he must face eternity, or the lack of it, each day."[27]

I was not a lonely writer, but I was and am alone in silence, solitude, when I write best. Normally I am a gregarious, talkative person and love to be with people, but not when I'm writing intently. In Assisi I learned to juggle both parts of my personality by writing in the morning, contemplating the city in the afternoon, and talking to the guests at breakfast, lunch, and dinner, plus on some evenings when someone would ask me to go for a walk down to the piazza. It worked well and was one of the many gifts Assisi gave me. It showed me how to write in solitude and silence and still be socially engaged with people I would meet for a brief time in Assisi where I lived during those charmed months.

Chapter Twenty-One
. . .

THE JOY OF BEING ELSEWHERE

FOR THE PILGRIM TRAVELER THE JOY OF ASSISI IS THE JOY OF being elsewhere. You are away from home, you enter an order made and maintained by someone else. Someone else is caring for all the details that weigh you down when you are at home. Like a lord or lady you are being served and attended to so that you can let go and surrender to the place itself. You can see what even those who live there cannot see or haven't taken the time to see. You can imagine the way it was when St. Francis and St. Clare walked the streets of this city—and then it is the thirteenth century, and all of the things of your own century that you take for granted aren't there and perhaps haven't even been imagined.

You can imagine, too, what is no longer there, like the high towers of the feudal lords who lived in the upper part of the city near the cathedral church of San Rufino and around the Porta San Giacomo a Muro Rupto. Wars and sieges and social change have brought down the nobility and their towers and democratized the city.

That leveling process began already at the time of St. Francis. The castle on the top of the hill, the Rocca Maggiore, was itself leveled when St. Francis was a young man at a time when the pope and emperor were distracted with one another and the emperor's representative, Conrad of Lutzen, was in nearby Spoleto surrendering Assisi to the papal representatives there.

The citizens of Assisi, in the meantime, were tearing down the castle of the Rocca Maggiore and using the stones to reinforce and expand the walls of a new city, an independent commune with its own government, its own elected mayor, and with the piazza in the center of the town, midway between the upper and lower parts of the city, as its seat of government. The "Piazza del Comune," they called it: the Piazza of the Commune, located where the growing power was located, namely, with the rising merchant class among whom was the wealthy cloth merchant, Pietro Bernardone.

As a boy, St. Francis was neither of the nobility, the so-called *majores*, the greater ones, nor of the poor, the *minores*, the lesser ones. He was of the merchant class, and his conversion involved leaving the merchant class, with its values of money and power—and greed for more money and power—to live among the *minores*, the lesser ones. There he founded a religious order of the Lesser Brothers, the Friars Minor.

His conversion meant that he had to leave Assisi altogether, to leave "the world," as he called it. He walked out of the city of his birth, went down the slope of Mount Subasio to the plain below where the outcasts, the beggars, and the lepers lived.

You learn these facts quite soon if you tarry for any length of time in Assisi because everything there is from the time of St. Francis's and St. Clare's youth. And so you see that even St. Francis's tomb is in a basilica, which was outside the original city walls when it was built. The basilica rests on the *Collis Infernus*, the "Hill of Hell," where a sort of medieval city dump was, where gallows were planted instead of trees, and where the bodies of criminals and outcasts were thrown into anonymous graves. And

Clare, too, lived with the Poor Ladies in the Monastery of San Damiano *outside* the city walls.

St. Francis and the early brothers lived in huts surrounding St. Mary of the Angels in the valley below Assisi. St. Francis called the place of their chapel and huts, the Porziuncola, the Little Portion.

You who learn these historical facts and see for yourself the geography of conversion know that beautiful, mystical Assisi is really for leaving, not staying. Here is where St. Francis learned that you cannot remain in the comfort and protective walls of your own making if you are to follow Jesus Christ who had nowhere to lay his head, as his Gospel proclaims. You must come out from behind your own comfort-producing walls, pass through the narrow gate, descend to where the poor dwell in despair, and try to make a difference there. You bring with you all the inspiration and mystical resonances that are still there in Assisi to go where you didn't go before: to those who haven't the freedom of travel you have, who haven't even the freedom to travel to another, higher part of the place where they live.

Assisi, then, is the tabernacle, the temple, that welcomes you, embraces you, inspires you, and then asks you to leave in the footsteps of St. Francis, who is following in the footsteps of Jesus, the Christ.

Assisi is reminder and symbol that if we are to follow Christ, we will symbolically leave the land of Ur, as Abraham did, and go into a land we do not know, led only by faith and trust that it is God who leads us, usually through deserts and over mountains, to a place that is foreign to us where a new way of living is waiting to be forged: a land where rich and poor, weak and strong, try to live in peace and work for justice.

This is utopian, of course. The real world is a land that is ever being made, but it is the making, the perseverance, that keeps us always outside those structures which keep trying to put walls around the poor and powerless, to exclude them from those who keep trying to deny them their rights, their very existence.

Assisi the beacon, the light on a hill that keeps sending us forth to where there is no light, except the light we carry with us, a light we found at the shrines of Francis and Clare who lived and died outside the walls where Christ lives among the poor, the lepers, and the outcasts.

To go to Assisi and tarry there for a while is to risk changing your life and passing out of its gates to a new life that will change how you live when you return to where you started from. To find Assisi is to find your home.

Chapter Twenty-Two

. . .

LONGING

IN 1988 WHEN THE UNIVERSITY OF CINCINNATI OFFERED ME a scholarship and fellowship to pursue a doctorate in English, I knew almost immediately that if my provincial minister approved, I would accept, even though this new direction would mean I would not be able to return to Assisi for at least four years, which is what happened.

And though I was drawn into and loved my doctoral studies and writing a book of poetry and short stories for my dissertation, the dream of Assisi remained strong within me. I wondered, not knowing where I would be hired after the completion of my studies, if I would ever return to that gleaming city on a hill in Umbria.

Bur four years later I did return to work at least one pilgrimage a year during the ten years I taught and was writer-in-residence at Thomas More College in Crestview Hills, Kentucky, across the Ohio River from Cincinnati.

And even when I retired from teaching, after thirty-six years in the classroom, Assisi has continued to be there, a lodestone drawing me back for at least a month every fall. It is one of those certainties we count on to be there always, even after we are no longer able to go there bodily.

I remember arriving in Assisi after those four academic years away. I went immediately to the Piazza del Comune and, putting down my luggage, plopped into a chair at the Bar Sensi, now Bar Bi, across the street from the fountain with its four lions spouting water and with pigeons always seemingly perched there, the very fountain where Francis and Bernard of Quintavalle distributed all of Bernard's possessions when he became Francis's first companion and Lesser Brother. As I sipped a cappuccino, I wondered if anyone would still remember me and if the city would have changed since last I sat in the Piazza del Comune.

The afternoon sun was still strong on the hot piazza stones and in my eyes, as before; but I didn't recognize anyone around me or anyone walking through the piazza. Those at the other tables looked like tourists or pilgrims deep into their own thoughts or conversations, and I felt something of a stranger to my own home until a taxi circling the fountain came to an abrupt stop, and Mauro Sannipola, a friend I'd known since he was a boy, honked his horn and waved and called out, "Stay there, I'll be back in a few minutes." And so it came to pass, and so I knew I was home again, talking to Mauro, listening to all the old news I'd missed, and breathing once more the clean air of Assisi.

What I realized as Mauro and I talked—and I noticed even black-clad older women talking on what seemed to me improbable cell phones—was that what matters remains, even though peripheral things such as cell phones and iPads, new fashions and upscale shops, are added to the equation of the Assisi experience. What remains is the city itself and one's own connection to it and its people. And even the people will pass one by one, and new friends will join the circle of one's friends. But the city will remain, its spirit, its essence unchanged by the ever-changing incidentals of modernity.

It is that spirit of place, the *genius loci,* that we long for when we "long to go on pilgrimage," as Chaucer puts it in the Prologue to his Canterbury Tales.

Longing. What was I really longing for when, those four absent years, I longed to return? Was it something in me, or out there beyond me—or both? I've come to believe that Assisi is something inside me that was awakened the first time I came to Assisi and lived for three months in its embrace. It was adventure, surprise, and a peace that came, I see now, from a sense of belonging in Assisi, a sense that this place was familiar, somewhere I'd been before, somewhere that was more a return than a discovery.

What we long for, I suppose, is the place where we began. I began my own spiritual life in Assisi years before I entered the city itself; for what began in Assisi with the birth of Francis Bernardone, brought me to a Franciscan high school seminary when I was fourteen years old. It was Assisi, far away in Italy, that drew me from Gallup, New Mexico, where I was born, to Cincinnati, Ohio, where I began a new life that would one day bring me to Assisi, where my new life really began.

We always seem to be longing for a home, even when we travel thousands of miles away from another home. We long to find the home that preceded the home where we were born into this world. I am not speaking of reincarnation, but of remembering the source of all longing: God, who in the Incarnation makes certain places holy by walking and living there or by his walking and living somewhere in his visitation to holy people like St. Francis who in turn make holy the place where God first came to them.

For Francis that place was and is Assisi and its environs. He is St. Francis of *Assisi*, the place where God again walked among us in St. Francis, the mirror of God's Son, Jesus Christ. Like the Holy Land of the Middle East, Assisi is the holy land of Umbria that awakened in me the origins of my own Franciscan spirituality. It is both origin and end, the place where someday the ashes of my memory will remain close to the place where remain the bones of him who awakened my inner life when I was fourteen years old and again when I was thirty-five and again and again and again…

Afterword
. . .

ALWAYS WITH LOVE, IT SEEMS, THERE IS THE RAIN. AND SO IT
WAS when I was finishing this homage to Assisi. It began to
rain, a soft, almost soundless rain that gathered all the scents of
the garden where I was writing and surrounded me with them:
ginestra, lime, geranium, fern, cypress. Even the otherwise scent-
less cactus plants seemed fragrant with rain. An omen of spring,
of a spiritual aroma that is Assisi, that is Francis and Clare, that
is whatever blooms and dies and blooms again over the centuries.
How can one not rejoice and praise God for Sister Water—and
praise God through her and with her.

As my life in Assisi began with rain so many years ago, so
this book ends with rain. With rain comes new life. It is raining
today here in Assisi. Tomorrow there will be sun.

Notes

. . .

1. *Mirror of Perfection,* in Murray Bodo, *Through the Year with Francis of Assisi* (Cincinnati: St. Anthony Messenger Press, 1993), p. 195.

2. *Anonymous of Perugia,* in Marion A. Habig, *St. Francis of Assisi: Writings and Early Biographies: English Omnibus for the Sources for the Life of St. Francis* (2 vols.) (Cincinnati: Franciscan Media, 2008).

3. Henry James, "Italian Hours," from *Collected Travel Writings: The Continent* (New York: Viking, 1993), p. 503.

4. Sophie Jewett, *God's Troubadour, the Story of St. Francis of Assisi* (New York: Thomas Y. Crowell, 1910), pp. 1–2.

5. Nikos Kazantzakis, *Report to Greco* (New York: Simon and Schuster, 1965), pp. 377–382.

6. Stanley Plumly, *Posthumous Keats* (New York: W.W. Norton, 2008), p. 342.

7. Bodo, *Through the Year with Francis of Assisi,* p. 57. Author's translation.

8. Linda Gregg, *In the Middle Distance* (St. Paul, Minn.: Graywolf, 2006), p. 54.

9. Rainer Maria Rilke, *New Poems,* trans. Edward A. Snow. (New York: North Point, 2001).

10. Thomas of Celano, Second Life, 214, in Bodo, *Through the Year with Francis of Assisi,* p. 186.

11. Sr. Frances Teresa Downing, O.S.C., trans. and notes, *Saint Clare of Assisi, Volume 2: The Context of Her Life* (Phoenix: Tau, 2013), p. 50.

12. Murray Bodo, *Francis: The Journey and the Dream* (Cincinnati: Franciscan Media, 2012), p. 227.

13. Sr. Frances Teresa Downing, O.S.C., trans. and notes, *Saint Clare of Assisi: Volume 1: The Original Writings* (Phoenix, Tau, n.d.), p. 35.

14. Downing, p. 35.

15. Downing, pp. 50, 53, 55.

16. Downing, p. 65.

17. Downing, p. 69.

18. Downing, pp. 85, 87, 88.

19. Downing, p. 89.

20. Quoted in "Israel Environment and Nature: Olive," www.jewishvirtual-library.org/jsource/Environment/olive.html.

21. Murray Bodo, *Wounded Angels* (Carlisle, U.K.: Blissfool, 2009), p. 45.

22. The whole of this story and more is detailed in Josef Raischl, S.F.O. and Andre Cirino, O.F.M., *Three Heroes of Assisi in World War II: Bishop Giuseppe Nicolini, Colonel Valentin Müller, Don Aldo Brunacci* (Phoenix: Tau, 2014).

23. Bodo, *Wounded Angels*, p. 47.

24. Paul Cronin, ed., *Herzog on Herzog* (London: Faber and Faber, 2003), page xx?

25. Thomas of Celano, *First Life of Saint Francis*, author's translation.

26. *The Economist*, February 1, 2014, obituary for conductor Claudio Abbado, died January 20, 2014, http://www.economist.com/news/obituary/21595387-claudio-abbado-conductor-died-january-20th-aged-80-claudio-abbado.

27. Ernest Hemingway, "Banquet Speech," www.nobelprize.org/nobel_prizes/literature/laureates/1954/hemingway-speech.html.

ABOUT THE AUTHOR

Murray Bodo, O.F.M., is a Franciscan priest and a member of the Franciscan Academy. An award-winning author of many books, including *Francis: The Journey and the Dream*, *Francis and Jesus*, *Landscape of Prayer*, and *The Simple Way: Meditations on the Words of Saint Francis*, he writes and lectures on Franciscan spirituality.

Printed in the United States
by Baker & Taylor Publisher Services